Secrets of the

HAREM

Carla Coco

THE VENDOME PRESS
New York   Paris

To Flavio

The Vendome Press
1370 Avenue of the Americas
Suite 2003
New York, NY 10019

Distributed in the U.S.A. and Canada by
Rizzoli International Publications
through St. Martin's Press
175 Fifth Avenue
New York, NY 10010

English translation © 1997 Philip Wilson Publishers and
The Vendome Press

Design Scibilia & Scibilia
Translated from Italian by Francesca White

Published in Italy in 1997 by
Arsenale Editrice srl
San Polo 1789
I – 30125 Venezia

Copyright © 1997
Arsenale Editrice

Library of Congress Cataloging-in-Publication Data
Coco. Carla.
        Secrets of the Harem / by Carla Coco.
                p.   cm.
        ISBN 0-86565-996-6
        1. Harem—Turkey. 2. Women—Turkey—Social
conditions. 3. Turkey—History—Ottoman Empire, 1288-
1918. I. Title.
HQ1726.7.C63 1997
305.42'09561—dc21   97-13595
                                                                CIP
ISBN: 0-86565-996-6

Printed in Italy by EBS – Editoriale Bortolazzi-Stei, Verona

Turkish spelling and pronunciation

Words and names from the Ottoman period have been
transcribed into modern Turkish, which is logical and
phonetic. Most letters are pronounced as in English, with
the following exceptions. Vowels are said as in French or
German; *a* as in "rather", *e* as in "let", *i* as in "machine",
o as in "oh", *u* as in "flute". The *í* is said as the *u* in "but",
ö as in German or as *oy* in "annoy", *ü* as in German or as
ui in "suit". Consonants are pronounced as in English,
except for:

ç   as *ch* in "china"
c   as *j* in "jam"
g   as *g* in "get" (hard), never as in gem
ğ   is almost silent and tends to lengthen the preceding
vowel
ş   sounds like *sh*, as in "sugar"
ïö   as in the French *êu* and the German *ö*
ü   as in the French *u* and the German *ü*

The illustrations are acknowledged in the captions. Those
from the following collections
Biblioteca Nazionale Marciana di Venezia
Biblioteca Palatina di Parma
Galleria Nazionale d'Arte Moderna di Roma
are reproduced with the permission of the Ministero per i
Beni Culturali e Ambientali.

CONTENTS

WOMEN OF THE OTTOMAN EMPIRE

The harem was a perquisite of the rich,
given that it was only they who were
able to maintain many women with
ease. The ordinary Turk had only one
legitimate wife, even though he was
allowed up to four, and one or
two concubines.
Stefano Ussi, *The Return of the Sheik*, 1856.
London, Chaucer Fine Arts.

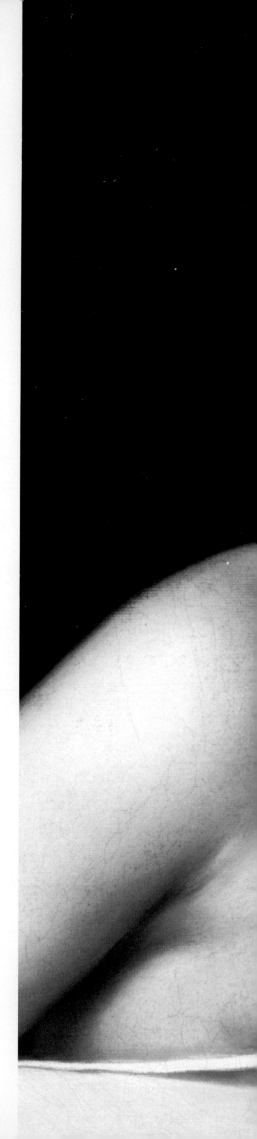

THE SOCIETY OF WOMEN

The complex structure of Ottoman society must be viewed from many angles in order to understand its true nature. This is particularly true of the situation of women in this society, which appears rich and varied only when one has penetrated the complex organization that governed it. Under the apparently rigid separation of the sexes in Turkey areas of freedom existed that cannot be perceived at first glance. The world of the Ottoman woman was like the facade of an Ottoman house: simple and unadorned, neglected and almost ugly, it gave no inkling of the luxury and refinement within the harem, the most intimate quarters of the home, that mysterious refuge rarely disturbed by the outside world. In the same way, under the uniform of their anonymous *ferace*, which rendered them invisible to the eyes of men, was concealed the welter of needs, desires, hopes and dreams of oriental women.

In Ottoman society, women were an integral part of the family, a notion that was acquired by the Turkish people only after the original tribes, held together by common ancestors, had settled and become urbanized. The extended family formed a nucleus, living under the authority of the *pater familias*. Father, mother, married and single sons, daughters, grandchildren, concubines, slaves and servants lived together under the same roof. But, following the custom of Islam, they were segregated, the men living in the *selamlik*, the women in the *haremlik*, the two distinct and isolated parts of an Ottoman household.

The father was the head of the household, and all members of the family owed him respect and obedience. He was in charge of the servants and the running of the household, but his wife reigned undisputed over the women's quarters. The harem was her domain and, to enter it, even the head of the family observed an etiquette that could not be disregarded except in the most exceptional circumstances. Thus, although in principle the man had all rights, in practice he was governed by moderation and generosity, qualities prescribed by the Koran and

The prayers recited by Muslims five times a day while facing in the direction of Mecca include ritual gestures and formulas which are repeated.
Giulio Ferrario, *Il Costume antico e moderno*, Milan, 1828. Venice, Biblioteca Nazionale Marciana.

Muslim law, which throughout the centuries had safeguarded the rights of all members of society.

The urge to settle, and imperial rule, meant that Turkish women lost the high social rank and freedom they had enjoyed on the steppes of Asia. With the reorganization of society came cultural changes in the nomadic nature of a people used to open spaces and to the magical-religious practices of shamanism, which culminated in ecstasy or the attainment of the cosmic journey. Islamic precepts and Byzantine customs imposed segregation in the harem on women and the loss of their active role in society. However, because of this nomadic inheritance, unlike women in the rest of the Islamic world, Turkish women were never completely marginalized in society, and they managed to contrive pockets of autonomy and, at certain moments in history, even to reverse their position of social inferiority.

The Koran permits a man to have four legitimate wives and an unspecified number of concubines, but it requires that they be maintained with a degree of decorum. It follows that only men of high rank – viziers, beys and pashas – possessed a harem, while most men were monogamous. As several Western travellers pointed out, during the course of his life a Turk saw only those five or six women who were part of his close family and had no other sexual outlet except to look at Greek and Armenian women, those from Pera and the few European women who came to the Ottoman Empire. Any other ideas about sex consequently remained mere phantoms or dreams. Marriage, a custom accepted by all Turkish subjects, was not practised by the imperial family. In fact, after the second half of the fifteenth century the sultans formed no legal unions and, with rare exceptions, coupled only with concubines. On the

Embroidery, song and dance were the indispensable accomplishments of Turkish women. But they also passed on to each other by word of mouth skills and knowledge, such as medicinal and paediatric practices, which went well beyond the scanty official education that they received.
Raccolta di 120 stampe, Venetiis, 1783. Venice, Biblioteca Nazionale Marciana.

facing page
Turkish princes started their education at a very early age. Their tutor attended the harem every day, but in order to ensure that he had no contact whatsoever with the women, his lessons were strictly supervised by the black eunuchs.
Turchia Album di 62 foto, n.d. Venice, Biblioteca Nazionale Marciana.

The views of Constantinople and its surroundings painted by the Venetian Pietro Bellò at the end of the nineteenth century quickly became so popular with the European community at Pera that Sultan Abdül Hamit II appointed Bellò official court painter.
Pietro Bellò, *Entering Constantinople*. Bassano del Grappa, Pinacoteca.

HIDDEN YET FREE

It is forbidden, for example, for a woman to enter the back rooms of a shop: she must remain where she can be seen from the street. She is forbidden to ride on a tram merely for enjoyment: she must get off at the end of the route and not immediately return the way she came. She is forbidden to attract the attention of passersby, to stop here, to go there, to stay more than a certain amount of time in any given place. It is easy to imagine whether these rules are obeyed and indeed whether it would be possible to enforce them. Then there is the matter of that blessed veil; originally devised as a safeguard for the male, it becomes the salvation of the woman, its hazy transparency arranged to entice, its folds to appease. Hence the most bizarre occurrences: fortunate lovers who after much time still do not know the identity of their beloveds; women who shelter under another's identity to wreak vengeance; jokes, recognitions, dupings, all of which give rise to endless gossip and squabbles.

De Amicis, *Costantinopoli*, 1878

other hand, the royal princesses were the only women in the Empire who, on marrying slaves, could impose monogamy on their spouses.

Women in Ottoman society acquired new status when they became mothers. A Muslim considered himself fulfilled only when he had descendants (preferably male), so maternity conferred privileges. Female sterility can thus be seen as one of the reasons for polygamy. In the harem of a great lord, as in that of the most humble household, mothers ruled their daughters, daughters-in-law, female servants and sons up to a certain age. Boys were educated outside the harem, but remained dependent on their mothers for many years. A mother chose her son's bride, when upon the death of the father, the son became head of the family and his wife the new mistress of the house. A son's attitude to his mother remained one of utmost deference. In the Sublime Porte, this devotion was fully revealed in the very great respect that was paid to the mother of the sultan, the *valide* sultan, in the titles bestowed upon her by which she was publicly addressed, and the power she retained after her spouse's death.

A Turkish man was privileged from birth. He was cherished and spoilt and, if he came from a bourgeois family, he was educated to become a civil servant in a *medrese*, or religious school; if from a family of merchants, he was educated to follow the family business. Girls were given

less education and, with rare exceptions, were brought up to be simply mothers and wives. They had to learn to cook and to undertake other domestic tasks, and if they came from a well-to-do family they had to learn to play a musical instrument, to embroider and to run a household. Despite these restrictions and the lack of formal education, Turkish women were skilled in the art of reciting poetry; they were acquainted with the use of medicinal herbs for the cure of illness and the preservation the body, knowledge that was handed on from one generation to the next.

In Ottoman society – as in European society of the time – a woman was brought up with matrimony as the ultimate goal. From the time of her birth the family prepared for this important event. Her mother selected and chose the groom, guided her daughters and carried out the complicated negotiation of an alliance, often after many preliminaries had taken place in the *hamam*, the public baths, which could be considered the drawing room of Turkish ladies. Following that, more private encounters occured in the harems, until the families reached an agreement, when the fiancé offered traditional gifts and gave the father of the bride a contribution towards the expenses of the wedding.

Matrimony was not only a sign of respectability and a social duty but also a financial transaction. The Koran stipulates the payment of a sum of money by the groom

The obligation to be totally covered when going out was in fact an advantage, for Ottoman women could see and not be seen and were free to move about unrecognized, without the fear of meeting inopportunely with a jealous husband or meddling family.
George De La Chappelle, *Rucuel de Divers Portrait*, Paris, 1648. Venice, Biblioteca Nazionale Marciana.

A balanced relationship between the different social groups in the Ottoman Empire allowed the peaceful coexistence of its many peoples of different languages, religions and cultures.
Turchia Album di 62 foto, n.d. Venice, Biblioteca Nazionale Marciana.

proportionate to his wealth, and this was kept by the bride in the event of repudiation. Repudiated wives were not social outcasts, and were taken back by their families. Repudiation, however, was the unilateral prerogative of the male and, in the event of conjugal misbehaviour, the woman's only recourse was to appeal to a judge, who instructed the transgressor in a more correct interpretation of his role of husband.

Turkish women could dispose of their property; that is, they were allowed to buy and sell within their means. Unlike a male heir, a woman had a right to only one half of the inheritance received by a man: but one must remember that in 'progressive' Europe of that time primogeniture was in force, so the position of Ottoman women seems almost enviable. Freedom for women was strictly related to their social standing. Lower-class women went to the market or the *hamam* unaccompanied; middle-class women were accompanied by a servant; ladies were accompanied by slaves and eunuchs; the favourites of the sultan were rarely seen in public and then only for a discreet outing, carefully arranged and under the strictest surveillance. Still, there were always ways and means to overcome the restrictions imposed by caste.

Turkish women were required to be scrupulously covered when they went out. The indispensable uniform was the *ferace*, a long and shapeless garment that came down to the ankles, and the *yaşmak*, a veil that covered the hair and the face leaving only the eyes visible. This perpetual mask, required by the menfolk to protect them from the temptation of the sight of a woman's face, turned out to be an advantage. Women could see and not be seen, move about incognito and, being invisible, do what they pleased. An upper-class woman who wished to visit the bazaar alone could easily transform herself into a common woman by putting on a crude *ferace*. It is in this way that Aziyadè, the heroine of one of Pierre Loti's novels, meets her European lover without running any risk. No husband could recognize his wife in the street, and even if he had the strongest suspicions, he could not confirm them, since it was not done for a Muslim to address a woman in a public place.

The veil and the harem suited the theatrical nature of the Turks. The streets of Constantinople provided a permanent stage on which an army of anonymous women paraded in operatic costume. The harem – closed, out of bounds, silent – provided a compelling reason for writing poetry, since the beloved would never hear the delicate verses and amorous sighs of the lover. In Europe many pages have been written on the subject of the enclosed universe of women's quarters, and the institution of the harem has been analysed from many points of view. But whether it is mythicized or decried, seen as a venue for refined

In the Ottoman world, which was free
from Christian puritanical attitudes,
the body was cosseted and nudity was
accepted without any false modesty.
Francesco Hayez, *La Bagnante*. Rome, Galleria
Nazionale d'Arte Moderna.

following pages
Giuseppe Aureli, like many other late
nineteenth-century painters, drew his
inspiration from prints and
photographs which were readily
available in Rome due to the craze for
things Turkish throughout Europe
at the time.
Giuseppe Aureli, *Gossip in the Harem*, London,
Mathaf Gallery.

erotic pleasures or an elegant girls' boarding school, the harem was an unsullied place where women could think, speak and get to know one another. In Europe, the right of a woman to demand an intimate, private place of her own was not regarded as seemly, and it was only at the beginning of the eighteenth century, in aristocratic circles, that the idea was entertained of providing apartments for the exclusive use of women. Lady Mary Wortley Montagu, the wife of Sir Edward Wortley Montagu, British ambassador in Constantinople at the beginning of the eighteenth century, attributed the ability of Ottoman women to create domestic and political pressure groups to this territorial freedom of the harem, and saw it as the factor that allowed them to create an anti-society, which alone was truly free in an empire of slaves.

Since the eighteenth century, Ottoman women, swept along on a wave of reform, became the interpreters of the process of modernization, which gradually modified their position. A wider culture, the influence of various writings, a comparison with European civilization as reported in the newspapers and, above all, their entry into the job market, where they had a precisely defined social role, brought about progressive female emancipation.

At the beginning of the twentieth century, with the dissolution and fall of the Ottoman Empire, many of its characteristic institutions also passed away. Polygamy and repudiation were abandoned, the harems were closed. A whole era came to an end, and with it the dreams, hallucinations and myths it had sustained.

A MEETING IN SALONIKA

I was so sure of being utterly alone that it gave me a strange feeling to become aware of a human head close beside me behind the thick iron bars, and of two huge green eyes fixed on me.

The eyebrows were dark, slightly frowning, almost touching; the expression in the eyes was a mixture of energy and ingenuity: a child's glance one might have thought, so full was it of freshness and youth.

The girl to whom the eyes belonged got up and revealed a figure to the waist enveloped in a Turkish garment with long and rigid pleats. The garment was of green silk, embroidered in silver. A white veil closely enveloped her head, revealing only her forehead and those huge eyes. The irises were really green, that sea green of which the poets of the Orient used to sing.

This maiden was Aziyadè.

Aziyadè was gazing at me fixedly. She would have hidden herself before a Turk, but a *giaur* is not a man: at the most he is an object of curiosity which one can contemplate at will. She seemed surprised that one of these foreigners who had come to threaten her country in terrible iron machines could be a very young man whose appearance caused her neither revulsion nor fear.

Loti, *Aziyadè*, 1871

---

following pages
Edouard Debat-Ponsan, *The Massage*, 1883.
Toulouse, Musée des Augustins.

In the late nineteenth century, upper-class women too, wore the fez, and clothes had become an opportunity for display, coquetry and extravagance.
Turchia Album di 62 foto, n.d., Venice, Biblioteca Nazionale Marciana.

facing page
A room in the baths of the seraglio with attendants wearing high wooden clogs inlaid with mother-of-pearl. A favourite Turkish pastime was to frequent the baths, bathe and be massaged and relax and gossip in pleasant surroundings.
Giulio Ferrario, *Il Costume antico e moderno*, Milan, 1828. Venice, Biblioteca Nazionale Marciana.

E. DEBAT-PONSAN
1883

A CLOSED AND PRIVATE PLACE

Ugly, deformed and fierce-looking,
black eunuchs from Africa were used
during the time of the
Ottoman Empire to guard the women
of the harem.
Jean-Léon Gérome, *The Guardian of the
Harem*, 1859. London, Wallace Collection.

THE SERAGLIO OF THE OTTOMAN SULTANS

facing page
Plan of Constantinople.
Cristoforo Buondelmonti, *Isolario*,
XV century. Venice, Biblioteca Nazionale
Marciana.

A valuable incense burner.
Istanbul, Topkapí.

A small triangular peninsula faces the golden city of Scutari and the infidels' quarter of Galata. It lies at the mouth of the Golden Horn, bathed by the warm waters of the Sea of Marmara and by the treacherous currents of the Bosporus. It was on the gentle slope of this remote and salubrious cape that Sultan Mehmet II chose to build his official residence in the second half of the fifteenth century.

At the beginning of the fourteenth century the Turks, a warlike nomadic people, had infiltrated the plateau of Anatolia and during the century had created a strong and awesome state inside the territory of the declining Byzantine Empire. Christendom considered these Knights of Altai as barbarians, seeing their progress toward Europe as an invasion that culminated in the conquest of Constantinople, the splendid capital of the Palaeologi and the Comneni. They entered the city after a long siege on 29 May 1453.

Mehmet II (1451–81) was not content with the realization of his cherished dream, the throne of the emperor. He wanted to create a new form of government, to reorganize the state and to leave his mark upon the city's architecture and arts. He was a stubborn and authoritarian man, but at the same time one who appreciated Greek culture and art, even breaking Koranic law in order to have Gentile Bellini paint his portrait. Mehmet carefully renewed and reconstructed Constantinople without breaking the link with Greek culture that connected the city with her past glory.

The place that was chosen for the construction of the first imperial residence was a densely populated area on the Third Hill, near the Forum of Theodosius. Once the building had been completed, Mehmet moved here with his court and his harem, but it soon became apparent that the palace was not suitable for the needs of the new Conqueror. For the sultan had restructured his court on the Byzantine model, thus considerably increasing the number of civil servants, pages, white eunuchs, servants and men of letters. As Conqueror, he preferred the complex Greek ceremonial to the more straightforward customs of Asia, and chose to distance himself from his subjects like a mighty lord. Writing some centuries later, Lady Mary Wortley Montagu noted with irony that this deliberate distancing was his first step towards achieving his ideal to become 'the most absolute of all monarchs who

Sartory

port. petrace   port. fidea

Vlacher na

Constant pnus

palatium Imperato

.S. b. de betm.

Apostol

S. Sophia

domus Justine na

petrus marf

Séto qua ranta

palatium impe ratoris Justi niani

S. Andreas

paralef teror.

porta inqui

S. Jannes despusio

portus Volanga

porta enesia

Constantinopolis olim Bizantium
urbis mett xvii

recognizes no other law than his own will'. As heirs to Byzantium, the Turks at that time seemed to require luxury, rigid hierarchy, elaborate ceremonial and a sublime loftiness.

Under the barbarian rule, there were many changes in Asia Minor. The Turkish Crescent waved above the lovely Byzantine basilicas, and on the ruins of Constantinople rose Istanbul, new city of wealth and beacon of Islam. Like Rome, the most vibrant and splendid metropolis of the East was built on seven hills. Mehmet chose the first of these on which to build his second palace.

At that time the site of the palace, known as *Saray Burnu*, the Cape of the Seraglio, was covered by trees and was easily defended from attack from sea or land. It was the perfect location for a medieval castle and was of historical importance, since it had once been the acropolis of ancient Byzantium. Work was begun by Mehmet in about 1459 and from then on, for four and a half centuries, every sultan made his own additions – a kiosk, a bath, a library – each addition contributing to the creation of the amazing labyrinth that we know today. The place is called Yeni Saray, the new palace, which Westerners call the seraglio, corrupting the word *saray*, which means palace. The earlier residence of Mehmet II near the Forum of Theodosius now became the Eski Saray, the old palace.

Travellers who visited the new Ottoman capital from the fifteenth century onwards were not, however, very impressed by this imperial palace and complained of its lack of majesty and the wretched materials used: the criteria of Turkish architecture

---

THE IMPERIAL HAREM

The silence of noon reigned over this mysterious palace which conceals behind the bars of its windows so much tedium, so much languishing. And I could not keep myself from thinking of all those treasures of beauty lost to the human eye, those wonderful examples from Greece, Circassia, Georgia, India and Africa, who vanished without any record having been made in marble or on canvas, without having been immortalized in art and left to the loving gaze of admirers throughout the centuries to come, those Venuses who will never have their Praxiteles, Violanti deprived of a Titian, La Fornarina never seen by a Raphael.

Théophile Gautier, *Constantinople*, 1853

The seraglio of the sultans in Constantinople was a complex of pavilions set in green surroundings and encircled by high walls. The Turks thought of a house as a tent and even imperial dwellings followed this concept.
Guer, *Moeurs et usages des Turcs*, Paris, 1746. Venice, Biblioteca Nazionale Marciana.

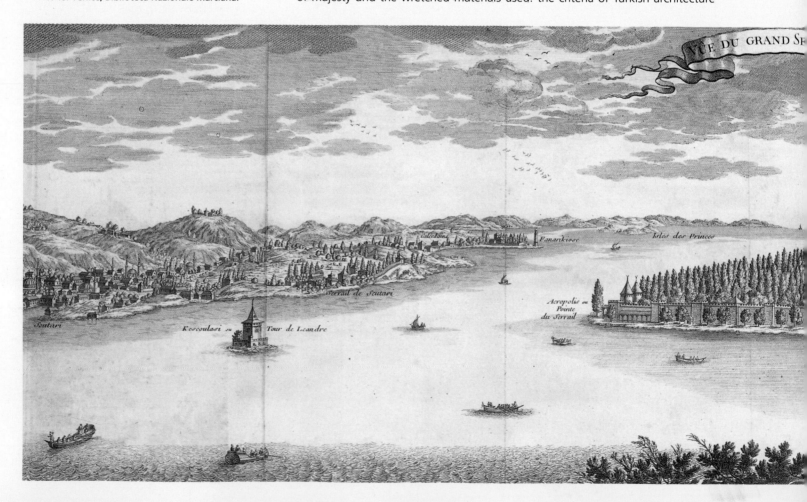

apparently escaped them. The Turkish aesthetic and notion of a dwelling were the direct opposite of European convention. Given their nomadic past, with its emphasis on the precariousness of life, the Ottomans adhered to the Islamic idea that a house is even less permanent than human life. What else is a dwelling than a tent on the steppes? Even the all-powerful sultans built their palace as a succession of pavilions, one distinct from the next, but all in total harmony with the surroundings.

The cape on which the seraglio was situated is like a natural citadel within the city, and it had been fortified in succession by the Greeks, Romans, Byzantines and Crusaders. When Mehmet II began construction of the palace, the Byzantine sea-walls were still in good condition, so the first task was to reinforce these and complete the circle of walls around the hill, with turrets at intervals guarded by soldiers and watchmen. At night the walls were defended by Janissaries, who did their rounds on a wheeled wooden platform, described by the Venetian ambassador Ottaviano Bon at the beginning of the eighteenth century in his detailed account of the palace. The guard was reinforced against a possible attack on the seaward side by a battery of cannon. Several gates break up the powerful, solid expanse of the external fortifications: twelve date back to the sixteenth century and eight or nine to the end of the eighteenth century. Almost all of them were service gates that were opened only by order of the sultan and for the daily business of the principal palace functionaries.

Wood was delivered to the Odun Kapísí, the Fuel Gate, facing the sea. A huge quantity was required for the palace, and a whole army of servants saw to its storage and unloading. Not far from this gate is Topkapí, the Cannon Gate, situated at a

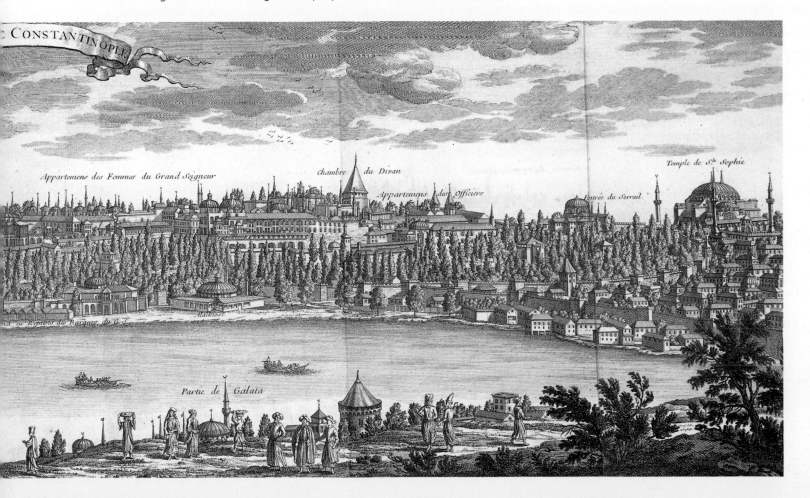

'The great pavilion of His Majesty, which encompasses many other pavilions, with vast halls, richly furnished, with porticoes, galleries, kitchens, stables and all other things; a small tower on one side, situated on a slight hill, with a place for the guards and a surrounded by great beauty.' Codice Cicogna, *Memorie turchesche*, XVII century. Venice, Biblioteca del Museo Correr.

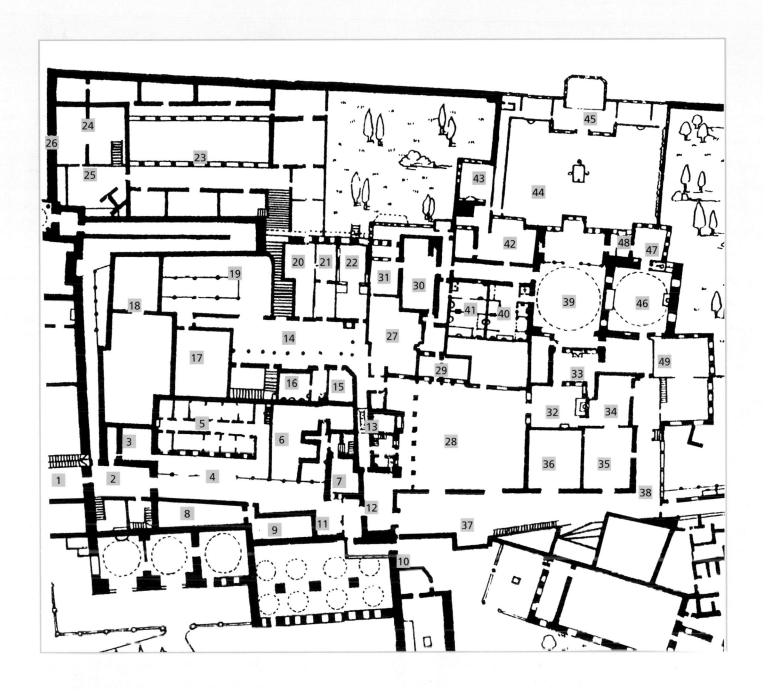

Key to map

1. Black eunuchs' Guard Room
2. Vestibule leading to the secret grille from behind which the sultan and the women could assist the council of ministers
3. Black eunuchs' mosque
4. Black eunuchs' court
5. Black eunuchs' quarters
6. School for the Royal Princes
7. Apartment of the chief of the black eunuchs
8. Lodgings for the harem's chief treasurer
9. Lodgings for the mistress of ceremonies
10. Gate of the Aviary
11. Principal gate of the harem
12. Black eunuchs' guard room
13. Slaves' quarters
14. Slaves' court
15. Slaves' kitchen
16. Slaves' baths
17. Slaves' dormitory
18. Harem laundry
19. Slaves' dormitory
20. Lodgings for the chief laundress
21. Lodgings for the supervisor of the novices
22. Lodgings for the nurse
23. Harem hospital
24. Lodgings for the hospital kitchen staff

25. Hospital kitchen
26. Gate of the Shawl
27. Sultan Ahmet's Kiosk
28. Sultana mother's Kiosk
29. Sultana mother's waiting Room
30. Sultana mother's dining Room
31. Sultana mother's bedroom
32. Room with a Hearth
33. Fountain Room
34. Harem Treasury
35. Apartment of the second, third and fourth wives of the sultan
36. Apartment of the sultan's first wife
37. The Golden Way
38. Consultation Place of the Jinns
39. Throne Room
40. Sultan's baths
41. Sultana mother's baths
42. Bedroom of Abdül Hamit I
43. Selim III's Room
44. Osman III's Court
45. Osman III's Kiosk
46. Murat III's great salon
47. Library of Ahmet I
48. Dining room of Ahmet III
49. Princes' Prison

The imposing Imperial Gate of the
Topkapí, between the fountain of
Ahmet III (right) and the basilica
of Hagia Sophia dominated by a
towering minaret.
Giulio Ferrario, *Il Costume antico e moderno*,
Milan, 1828. Venice, Biblioteca Nazionale
Marciana.

strategic point at the tip of the cape and flanked by two enormous cannon. Two square towers were built on each side in the seventeenth century, their military presence barely softened by the cypresses in the gardens that overlook them. The cannons were used to announce important public and religious events, rather than for defence against possible attack. As time went on, this gate came to give the entire palace its name, Topkapí Sarayí, the Palace of the Cannon Gate. Opposite, in the Sea of Marmara, were anchored two imperial caiques, ready to set out on a trip up the Bosporus or to the Islands of the Princes at the whim of the sultan – either on his own or in the company of his favourites.

The starkness of the walls was interrupted by several kiosks, where the sultan relaxed with his concubines or where he received court dignitaries. These small buildings, such as the rectangular Marble Kiosk near the Cannon Gate, which stood on pillars and was free of all decoration, were erected on flat ground or on natural hillocks and were surrounded by huge gardens full of exotic flowers and fruit trees.

Next to the ruins of the Byzantine church of Saint Demetrius, the Degirmen Kapí, was the Mill Gate, also known as the Halastar Kapísí, the Gate of the Sick, because it was used for the servants' hospital as well as for the bakery. The Demir Kapí, or Iron Gate, was used by officials and foreign dignitaries arriving by sea, and close by was the Kiosk of Pearls, built in 1582 by Sinan Pasha, Murat III's grand vizier. The Balík Hane Kapísí, the Fish Gate, led to the quarters of the fishermen employed by the court

The Akhor Kapí, the Stable Gate, led to vast stables, which housed three to four thousand horses. Towards the interior of the palace one found the Gülhane Kapí, which led to the gardens; the Soğuk Çeşme Kapísí, the Gate of the Fountain, built by Sultan Ibrahim in the mid-seventeenth century; the Onluk Kapí, or Gate of the Ten, used solely by the guards; and another gate, the Demir Kapí (not to be confused with the Sea Gate) that led to the gardens. All access through these gates was strictly regulated and limited to palace staff, but the main gate leading to the palace was open to all. It is known as the Bab-í Hümayün or Imperial Gate and stands about a hundred metres from the Hippodrome and the basilica of Hagia Sophia. It was originally adorned by an imposing white marble arch that created an impression of majesty and wealth. Above the entrance was a room which had various uses over the centuries. At the time of Mehmet II it was a private kiosk; under his son Beyazit II it was a storeroom for the possessions of those who had died without heirs; during the reign of Süleyman it was used by the women of the harem as a place from which to watch parades without being seen. In the seventeenth century strange little round turrets were added to the roof as ornaments, but eventually both the room and the turrets disappeared and only the niches remained at the sides of the door. These were used to display the severed heads of disgraced dignitaries as an example and a warning to the population.

The First Court of the Imperial Palace was open to all: Muslims and infidels, high-ranking dignitaries and the lower classes, the sultan's subjects and Christian visitors. However, admittance to the palace in no way diminished the vast distance between the sultan and his subjects, and the demarcation in the seraglio was quite

One of the sultan's guards.
Below. The fountain of Ahmet III with the Imperial Gate of the Topkapí in the background, photographed at the beginning of the twentieth century.
Turchia Album di 62 foto, n.d. Venice, Biblioteca Nazionale Marciana.

distinct. The outside public section, known as the *birun*, housed the government offices, while the *enderun* in the interior was the residence of the court, the harem and the sultan. The palace was representative of the 'circle of parity' that lay at the heart of the Ottoman Empire. All the essential elements of the state – the military, government officials, the court, the women, and lastly the sultan, absolute master of all and dispenser of all things and all happiness – were contained in concentric circles.

The chief of the Imperial Guards, whose function was to watch over the gates of the Imperial Palace, with his assistant. *Foggie diverse del vestire de' Turchi,* XV century. Venice, Biblioteca Nazionale Marciana.

The residential quarter was divided in the oriental manner; its four courtyards were kept rigorously separate by walls. The first courtyard, a huge unpaved open area, was for the horses of those arriving at the palace, and fifty *kapici*, or guards, armed with arquebuses, arrows and scimitars, controlled the entrance and kept an eye on the visitors. On the right side of the courtyard stood a long row of buildings that constituted the infirmary, which was under the jurisdiction of the head of the white eunuchs. The sick, in the care of two doctors and two surgeons, were housed in different apartments according to their type of illness. The sultan himself frequently visited the hospital, which was always full to overflowing, since many who were not ill had themselves admitted on some pretext of sickness because, according to Tavernier writing in 1682, it was reasonably easy to get hold of wine there. A rather odd regulation allowed those who managed to sneak in the forbidden alcohol not only to go unpunished but actually to drink it in the presence of the sultan himself, thus making a mockery of Koranic prohibitions. Quite a few of the seraglio servants were involved in the traffic in wine that took place in the neighbourhood of the hospital. On the left of the First Court was the arsenal

The First Court of the Topkapí. On the right is the hospital, a long row of low buildings. On the opposite side are the mill, the bakery and the church of St Irene. The cupolas of the mint and the goldsmiths' workshops stand out in the background. The court was open to the public, but many Janissaries kept order and watched over the behaviour of visitors.
Ignaz Melling, *Voyage pittoresque de Constantinople et du Bosphore*, Paris, 1819. Parma, Biblioteca Palatina.

facing page
The Ottoman court included many functionaries and servants. In the row above are the *ağa*, or chief commander, of the Janissaries, in ceremonial and ordinary uniform, the superintendent and the page of the *ağa*.
Giulio Ferrario, *Il Costume antico e moderno*, Milan, 1828. Venice, Biblioteca Nazionale Marciana.

The chief Janissary with a page. These young men, forcibly recruited from the Christian provinces of the Empire, converted to Islam and separated from all family and cultural ties, were the most fanatical supporters of the sultan.
Foggie diverse del vestire de' Turchi, XV century. Venice, Biblioteca Nazionale Marciana.

of the Turks, who kept their arms in what had been the Christian sanctuary of the Divine Peace, the ancient Byzantine church of St Irene, built by Constantine or by his son Constantius Clorus on a site previously occupied by a temple dedicated to Aphrodite. The courtyard also housed the *acemi oğlan*, young pages of Christian origin forcibly recruited from the outposts of the Empire, who were destined for the most humble duties. Two other buildings, a mill and a bakery, produced different grades of flour and bread that was distributed according to rank. On the opposite side was the mint with its cupolas, which was moved here from its original position on the Third Hill sometime before 1695. The mint also housed the workshops of goldsmiths, who crafted sumptuous decorations for the imperial apartments and fashioned rich adornments for the women of the harem. In the farthest corner was the aqueduct that supplied the entire Topkapí.

The First Court was also called the Court of the Janissaries, for apart from its many other uses it served as an assembly point for this awesome force, which Sultan Orhan Gazi had formed at the beginning of the fourteenth century and which had since become the right arm of the monarch. Janissaries were young men recruited from the Christian population. Torn from their families, uprooted from their culture, hardened through great privation, these soldiers were among the most faithful to the sultan. This *devşirme* system, feared and criticized by Westerners, was a major contributing factor in the creation of Ottoman power. The Janissaries used to gather under the plane tree in the courtyard; the names of their officers were linked to the culinary arts and their symbol was a cauldron (*kazan*), which they would turn upside down as a signal for revolt.

The Second Court was separated from the first by a majestic circle of walls, interrupted by the Bab-üs Selam, the Gate of Salutations, also known as the Middle Gate. Its date is uncertain, but it undoubtedly belongs to the early nucleus of buildings, and its crenellations and side towers constructed in the fifteenth century give it a medieval appearance. The fifty guards on duty enforced complete silence, the highest form of respect in the East. Even the most lofty dignitaries had to dismount here and proceed on foot, since only the sultan could enter on horseback.

The Court of the Divan, as it was known, was a tranquil place, with beautiful great fountains, paths bordered by tall cypresses and lawns with gazelles grazing on them. The elegance of the courtyard did not diminish its air of mystery, and the beauty of the buildings did not dissipate the terror inspired by the prison cells, where those no longer in the sultan's favour were languishing. The larger waiting room on the right-hand side, between the two doorways, reserved for foreign ambassadors and other important guests, was also a fearsome place; quite

frequently visitors were left waiting for hours and even days as a demonstration of the sultan's power.

The quarters of the government, the state functionaries, the halberdiers, as well as the kitchens, were also in the Court of the Divan. Through the Meyyit Kapísí, the Gate of the Dead, on the left-hand side were carried the bodies of those who died in the palace. The mosque of Beşir Ağa, the chief black eunuch in the mid-eighteenth century, faced on to an open court, as did the lodgings of the halberdiers, part of the external staff of the seraglio who acted as woodcutters and personal bodyguards for the inhabitants of the harem. Farther back was the sultan's private stable for twenty or thirty of his favourite horses. Above the stables were kept the trappings: saddles, bridles, breast-collars. This rich collection, beautifully adorned with a variety of jewels, was the wonder of Western visitors. A permanently locked door, constantly supervised by the black eunuchs, led to the forbidden women's quarters.

Next to this, under a vast portico, was the Kubbealtí, or Council Chamber, in which the council of ministers met. It was only a medium-sized room but most lavishly decorated with an oriental profusion of gold and jewels to create a lavish chromatic effect. Here the highest government decisions were taken and the council could be observed by the sultan, hidden behind a window with a grille that was symbolically positioned above the head of the grand vizier. The decoration on the Tower of the Divan, next to the hall, was also splendid. Both buildings were damaged by fire in 1574, and the restoration, carried out a short while later, failed to recreate the splendour that was the hallmark of Süleyman the Magnificent's reign. Next to the Divan was the Chancellery, or *Deftarhane*, where imperial decrees were drafted, the private office of the grand vizier, and the Inner Treasury, or *Hazine*.

The left wing of the courtyard formed a self-contained world, entirely taken up by the kitchens and lodgings of the household staff. After the fire of 1574 the area was rebuilt by Sinan, the great Janissary architect, on the same site as the original buildings erected by Mehmet II, the Conqueror. There were two mosques, baths, warehouses, offices, meeting halls and rooms for the use of the cooks, pastry cooks, and other kitchen staff, whose lifestyle was very different from that of the other servants in the palace.

The ten kitchens were reduced to seven at the end of the seventeenth century. The first was used only for the sultan; the second for his mother, wives, sisters and children; the third for the chief black eunuch, the director of the women, and the other black eunuchs; the fourth for the grand master of the seraglio and other officials; the fifth for the chief treasurer and his officials; the

facing page
The Council Chamber at the Topkapí where ministers met. Above the head of the grand vizier, who sits in the centre, is the grille behind which the hidden sultan participated at the meetings. An absolute ruler, he could depose at will any minister or functionary who displeased him.
Codice Cicogna, *Memorie turchesche*, XVII century. Venice, Biblioteca del Museo Correr.

A royal knight and his attendant. A strong military organization had allowed the Turks to create a vast and very rich empire.
Foggie diverse del vestire de' Turchi, XV century. Venice, Biblioteca Nazionale Marciana.

sixth for the chief cup bearer and his minions, and so on. The number of staff was reduced as time went by, but in the golden age of the Empire the kitchens employed three thousand people who, on a regular basis, prepared over six thousand meals a day, using vast quantities of beef, lamb, kid, mutton, chicken, pullets, pigeons, rice and butter.

The Bab-üs-Saadet, or Gate of Felicity, led into the Third Court. This marked the limit of the public area of the palace, with the exception of the *Arz Odasí*, the Throne Room, a small pavilion with precious marble and gold ornamentation, where foreign ambassadors were received. In accordance with Byzantine ceremonial, these diplomats were supported under the arms by two servants and led forward to kiss the robe of the sultan, who was seated on a magnificent throne. The Lord of the Turks sat hieratic and remote, with his hands hidden in the sleeves of his caftan, his gaze fierce and grave. He would not utter a word, and a nod of approval would be a sign of great benevolence. There were no guards at the Bab-üs-Saadet, only eunuchs in submissive postures. This door, with its vault and marble arches probably dating back to the sixteenth century, was also known as the Door of the White Eunuchs. The threshold was kissed by all who entered, since in the East the doorway possessed a mystical significance: indeed, the Ottoman Empire itself is referred to as the Sublime Porte.

This part of the residence was reserved exclusively for the sultan, his women and servants. To the right of the entrance were the lodgings of the white eunuchs and on the left was the apartment of the chief white eunuch, the *kapí ağasí*, whose duties were of the highest importance and who enjoyed the confidence of the sovereign. There were several pavilions in this courtyard, all built at different times; they included the main libraries of the seraglio – the Library of Ahmet III, for instance, in which were kept manuscripts of inestimable value, such as precious works on the history of Byzantium, and a new library known as the Yeni Kütüphane. Most of the courtyard was taken up by the palace school, with classrooms, common rooms, dormitories, baths and so on. Those youths who showed promise received an extensive education here, studying in depth religion, literature, such Islamic languages as Arabic and Persian, astronomy and the sciences. The youths, who had been forcibly recruited through the *devşirme* system, studied with the royal princes and, up to the disintegration of the Empire, shared all courses of study and leisure with them. They were called the *iç oğlan*, the boys of the internal household, and formed an elite group who were eventually selected for high office and the most prestigious positions in the Empire.

Another building was the treasury, next to which was the dispensary, or Kiler Koğuşu, where all sorts of drugs and spices were carefully preserved, including syrups, ground unicorn horn, theriacus and rue (antidotes against poison), among many others.

In a special pavilion, the Hirkai Şerif Odasí, were kept the 'most holy things', sacred relics of the Islamic faith. The sultan, 'The Shadow of God upon Earth', held the office of caliph and was, therefore, the head of the Sunni community. There were certain obligations related to this position, and the monarch had the privilege

The chief of the white eunuchs in the service of the sultan. The Ottoman Turks inherited from the Byzantines the custom of having eunuchs in their service at court, but since Islam forbade castration, they employed Christian or Jewish merchants to perform this operation. At first only white slaves were castrated, but from the sixteenth century blacks were preferred, since they were more resilient to the mutilation.
Raccolta di 120 stampe, Venetiis, 1783. Venice, Biblioteca Nazionale Marciana.

facing page
The Throne Room used for audiences with foreign ambassadors and, *below*, the Second Court of the Topkapí with the Gate of Felicity that leads into the Third Court.
Giulio Ferrario, *Il Costume antico e moderno*, Milan, 1828. Venice, Biblioteca Nazionale Marciana.

of keeping in his palace the most important objects connected with the Prophet: a piece of his tooth; a hair from his beard; the footprint in marble of his right foot; the cloak brought all the way from Cairo by Sultan Selim I in 1517 after the conquest of Egypt.

Farther into the palace it became increasingly a private residence, where the life of the sultan's harem, in luxurious and spacious surroundings, was shielded from prying eyes. Empty spaces were more frequent than filled spaces, and reflections of kiosks of coloured marble dissolved in water, surrounded by exotic gardens. The Pavilion of Erivan, or Rivan Köşkü, also called the Room of the Turban, or Sarík Odasí, provided the sultan and his companions with incomparable views over the changing waters of and activity in the Sea of Marmara and the Bosporus. It was built by Sultan Murat IV in 1635 after a long military campaign in the distant city of Erivan, where, it is said, the sultan saw a kiosk so lovely that he wanted it to be built in his royal garden. This building rivalled the nearby pavilion of Baghdad, the Baghdad Köşkü, built as a memento of another military victory. The two buildings, used by the sultans as reading or smoking rooms, places for the purposes of entertaining and for their times of relaxation, were separated by a splendid terrace made from fine marble, the Sultan Ibrahim Kameríyesí, which was enhanced by the presence of a large pool, or *havuz*, at the centre of an enchanting big water garden. Here the sultan and his favourite concubines would spend many hours of the day bathing and playing in the water.

At the edge of the terrace, there was a small balcony with a bronze canopy, facing the sea and known as the Iftariye; it was here that Sultan Ibrahim used to be served with his evening meal during the fast of *Ramadan*. From it he also dispensed the ritual alms during the sumptuous celebrations that accompanied the circumcision of his sons. Indeed, the *Sünnet Odasí*, used exclusively for the ceremonies and rites of the circumcision of the royal princes, is just next door.

On the gentle slopes below the terrace, the rococo kiosk of Mustafa Pasha, the Sofa Köşkü, and the Hekimbaşí Odasí stood out among the green and gold of the orange groves. The tower of the Hekimbaşí Odasí dated all the way back to the time of the Conqueror and had more the appearance of a prison than of a place that had been allocated for the use of the head tutor. A little farther on is the Mecidye Köşkü, the kiosk of Abdül-Mecit I, one of the last buildings to be erected in the palace. This kiosk was designed in the mid-nineteenth century by a French architect and shows the extent of the attraction that French culture had established for the last sultans.

Traditional Turkish homes were separated in two. The *selamlík*, the external area, almost an ante-chamber used for public affairs, was where the master of the house received visitors and friends; the *haremlík*, the heart of the home reserved exclusively for the women, was a mysterious refuge into which no stranger was allowed and where a life of pleasure and intimacy was lived. This division also existed in the House of Felicity of the Ottoman sultans, where the sumptuous royal apartments were joined to the women's quarters by an intricate maze of vestibules and passages.

These private apartments were built at different times according to the taste and the requirements of the various sultans who came after Mehmet II. The rooms were interconnecting: the Room with a Hearth, the Ocaklí Oda, which was built in 1665 after a fire, led into the richly decorated Fountain Room, the Çesmeli Sofa. This, in turn, led to the Hall of the Emperor or Royal Hall, the Hünkâr Sofasí, decorated with blue tiles and furnished with Chinese porcelain vases, Venetian mirrors and Empire-style furniture in a deliberate mixture of French and oriental styles. In this room the sultan took his pleasure with the favourites from the harem, listening to music, or enjoying singing and dancing or conversation. The women were seated apart, hidden behind the columns in a raised section of the room. The musicians, who came from outside the seraglio, played in the gallery, while the sultan sat on a canopied throne to the right.

To the left, beyond the corridor known as the Hamam Yolu, lay the royal baths, or Hünkâr Hamamí, while to the right were the bedroom of Sultan Abdül Hamit I, decorated in an unusually eccentric rococo style, and the more sober room of Selim III, which was furnished in the Turkish manner with low divans and lighted by a series of windows that look out on the gardens. From this room a passageway led

facing page
An exquisite Koran holder.

Koran stands with delicate intarsia decoration.
Istanbul, Topkapí.

following pages
The eclectic magnificence of the Topkapí Royal Hall, furnished with Chinese vases, Venetian mirrors and Empire-style furniture. At the accession of each sultan all the decorations of the harem were changed to satisfy the taste of the new sovereign.

to the kiosk of Osman III, built on the outer walls of the palace with a wide view over the Golden Horn and the Bosporus. This pavilion had Italianate exterior columns and an Ottoman-style roof; inside, it was divided into three rooms and richly decorated with tiles and frescoes showing Italian vistas, while the style of the furniture was French.

Behind the Hall of the Emperor was the great salon of Murat III, the walls tiled with elegant panels decorated with flower designs and topped with cornices. The murmur of a constant stream of water from a three-tiered fountain delighted the ears of the sultan and muffled the sound of voices outside. This room led to the small but charmingly furnished Library of Sultan Ahmet I, and next to this was the dining room of Sultan Ahmet III, the smallest in the seraglio, with the walls

facing page
Ottoman dance required great skill and created a grand spectacle. Wrapped in garments so thin that they allowed 'all the secret parts' to be revealed, the dancers used movements and gestures so lascivious as to 'liquefy marble', wrote a Venetian diplomat fortunate enough to have assisted at a performance.
Vincenzo Marinelli, *The Dance of the Bee in the Harem.* 1862. Naples, Museo di Capodimonte.

Detail of a wooden panel with fruit designs in the dining room of Ahmet III, the smallest room of the Topkapí.

entirely covered by wooden panels decorated with fruit and flowers. In the middle of the room, on a huge inlaid tray, stood a glass bowl containing fruit, and the cutlery used at meals.

But the Imperial Palace, a place of pleasure and delight, also had an apartment called the Kafes or Cage, which evokes images of the cruelty and misery caused by the depravity of the Sublime Porte during the long years of its decline. A long corridor, known as the Consultation Place of the Jinns, led to a dismal space, enclosed by walled-up doors and windows and completely sealed off by very high walls. Here lived the younger brothers of the sultan, the Turkish princes, who would not be allowed to inherit the throne. The law of fratricide, which existed for many centuries, authorized the reigning sovereign to eliminate his brothers. The killing had to take place without bloodshed, so had to be done either by strangulation or suffocation, to safeguard against the terrible consequences of such a heinous deed. The death sentence was eventually considered too cruel and was converted to life imprisonment in the Kafes. In consequence, in this remote corner of the House of Felicity lived the princes, who were brought up in total isolation by deaf mutes and women who had been forcibly sterilized. Here they endured many years in a state of terror that frequently gave way to madness; more rarely, they found comfort in a belief in the one true God who would be sure eventually to grant peace and freedom.

This great palace was a reflection of a huge and varied empire, the throne of the Ottoman sultans who, for many centuries, held Christendom in check, thanks to a judicious mixture of terror, diplomacy, statesmanship and military power. When in the mid-nineteenth century Topkapí was abandoned for a new palace on the Bosporus – the Dolmabahçe Palace, built in emulation of Versailles – the Knights of Altai had reached the end of their long march, and the Heavens no longer bestowed their favours on the 'King of Kings, Dispenser of Crowns to the Monarchs of the World, The Shadow of God on Earth'.

facing page
Detail of the elegant ceramics covering
the walls in the bedroom of Murat III.
Istanbul, Topkapí.

The three-tiered fountain in the
chamber of Murat III was built to
soothe the sultan with its rippling
water and at the same time to deaden
the sound of voices outside.
Istanbul, Topkapí.

HAREM, THE FORBIDDEN CITY

All Europeans travelling to the East were fascinated by the exotic voluptuousness they found. The Turk's strange sexual behaviour, the possibility of having four wives and numerous slaves to satisfy every whim, was reason enough to enflame the imagination. Turkish women were always seen in recumbent poses, lying on divans in rooms luxuriously appointed in Eastern splendour, or draped in whirling veils which covered them from head to foot when they ventured out on to the street. They were held to be the epitome of lustfulness and dishonesty. Europeans were captivated by this faceless, mysterious, fleeting world; by the subtle game of hide and seek which allowed them to imagine the woman however they wished, creating their own image of her.

The most voluptuous place in the Empire was the seraglio of the sultan. Of all the harems – and it must be remembered that these were appurtenances of all men of social standing – the harem of the great lord was unrivalled in size and quality. Before the conquest of Constantinople the women's quarters were at Edirne, the lovely city in the Thracian plain built by the Roman emperor Hadrian in 125 BC. Here, on a small island in the river Maritsa, was the palace of Mehmet II, surrounded by fabulous landscaped gardens, fruit trees and welcome shady nooks.

When the sultan moved to Istanbul with his court and women, the latter were housed in a part of the seraglio built on the Third Hill next to the Forum of Theodosius, and when Mehmet the Conqueror made Topkapí his official residence some ten years later, the women continued to live in the old seraglio. This decision reflected the sultan's strong desire to highlight the demarcation between public and private life at court. The old palace near the Forum was surrounded by high walls. Its many buildings housed a good number of people and it was furnished with fountains, cisterns, baths and luxuriant gardens, all for the well-being of the ladies. There was also the *mâbeyin*, the private apartment used by the sultan when from time to time when he wished to be with one of his favourites. Many contemporary travellers confirmed these details and stressed the fact that Turkish men did not live with their women, despite the fact that they possessed many girls of every age and condition: slaves, princesses, Christians and Europeans, renegades and Muslims.

In the sixteenth century, during the reign of Süleyman, known to

Tobacco and opium helped the women of the harem to pass the long night vigils filled with memories of the past, and to dispel their present fears and anxieties for the future.
Costumi orientali, XVII century. Bologna, Biblioteca Comunale dell'Archiginnasio.

Europeans as 'The Magnificent' and whom the Turks call 'The Legislator', the Ottoman Empire reached the apex of its military and political power and revitalized the laws, customs and public life of its society. Unwilling to let others dictate to him, and resolutely serious in the matter of government, Süleyman showed a desire to reverse the policy of separating public and private life inaugurated by his predecessor Mehmet II. As vulnerable in his affections as he was unassailable in matters concerning government, this sultan took as his friend a slave called Ibrahim, who had been a Christian and who became a powerful grand vizier. Then the sultan became attached to a charming, rather than beautiful, young Russian woman called Hürrem or Roxelana. A contemporary writer, Luigi Bassano, commented on the great love of the sultan for this girl, which left his subjects quite amazed. So strong was this attachment that in Constantinople it was thought she was a witch and that the sovereign had fallen under a spell.

New customs brought changes to life at court and in 1541 Süleyman allowed the women to be moved to the Topkapí. The event was expedited by a fire which broke out in the old seraglio, which, from that time onward, was used to house the women of a deceased sultan and the elderly women from former reigns. At first only Roxelana was installed, with about a hundred ladies and servants, but gradually the rest of the court, about three hundred women, were moved to the new seraglio. In the second half of the century, during the reign of Selim II and the Venetian sultana Cecilia Baffo-Venier, this arrangement became permanent. From that time, until the mid-nineteenth century, the imperial harem was not moved again. Thanks to the tales of luxury from *The Thousand and One Nights*, with their stories of mysteries, cruelties and contradictions, the Topkapí became the embodiment of a mythical place of delight and luxury which many dreamed of, some described and none ever knew.

From Süleyman's time onward, the women's quarters were continuously developed. As in the rest of the palace and perhaps even more so, these apartments were transformed every time a new ruler mounted the throne. The women of the deceased sultan were cleared out and sent off on their sad journey to the Palace of Tears, the old seraglio. The rooms were then redecorated and decked out with new furniture: divans covered in cashmere, Persian carpets, tables with mother-of-pearl inlay, fountains made of Marmara marble, Chinese porcelain, Venetian mirrors and French armchairs, creating an ever-changing atmosphere of intimacy and mystery, which reflected the taste and whims of the new master.

Changes were not only the result of a natural course of events but also of fires which ravaged the palace throughout the centuries. Such calamities were accepted as an almost natural occurrence in a city almost entirely constructed of wood, where fire regularly swallowed up entire districts. Monumental architecture was less prone to similar catastrophes, but even so the Imperial Palace was swept by a devastating conflagration in the spring of 1574. The fire started in the kitchens, and assisted by the cooking fats, spread quickly, soon reaching the harem. The whole area was restored to its original state by the architect Sinan. In 1665 a suspicious fire started in the women's quarters and the damage was even greater, since entire buildings were destroyed in addition to all the wooden structures.

The public area of the Topkapí was separated by a wall from the forbidden city. There were two main doors, the first of which, the Araba Kapísí, or Carriage Gate, led into a second courtyard, where the covered carriages awaited the ladies to escort them outside for a rare outing or to take them to Hadrianopolis, a favourite summer resort of the Ottoman sultans. Beside the entrance was an antechamber known as the Dolaplí Kubbe, a severe and unadorned place with scanty lighting, where two black eunuchs kept guard, day and night. They belonged to the large group of *castrati* in charge of the women, 'monsters without sex' as Théophile Gautier defined them. For the most part they came from the African provinces and had elegant names that contrasted starkly with their monstrous appearance. The antechamber led into a vestibule decorated with seventeenth-century ceramics from Kütahya. On the right a small room with a staircase led to the famous screen behind which the sultan, and at a later date the women once they had acquired power, watched in secret the meetings of the council of ministers.

Strategically arranged along the internal courtyard were the sleeping quarters of the black eunuchs, the *Harema ağalar Dairesi*, on three floors of narrow stuffy bedrooms with a small mosque. Next to these was the school for the royal princes, where the sons of the sultan were educated until they were eleven years old. Next came the apartment, complete with a bedroom, an office and general services, of the *Kízlara ağasí Dairesi*, the chief of the black eunuchs, a most important functionary in the imperial harem and the right arm of the *valide* sultan (sultan's mother). The apartments of two other important and privileged women – the chief treasurer of the harem, the *Hazinedar Dairesi*, and the mistress of ceremonies, the *Musahiban Dairesi*, – faced on to the opposite side of the courtyard.

At other end of the courtyard, in the *Nöbetyeri*, was stationed another body of guards made up of black eunuchs next to the second entrance to

SÜLEYMAN THE MAGNIFICENT
'SHADOW OF GOD ON EARTH'

'His Highness The Lord called Süleyman is tall in stature, thin, with an aquiline nose and a long neck. His complexion is wan, he is healthy and of a strong arm.' The Magnificent, son of Selim I and Hafsa Hatun, born on 6 November 1494 in Trebizond on the shores of the Black Sea, was thus described by his contemporaries as a benign and melancholic man. He grew up in this last stronghold of the Comnenus and gave himself wholeheartedly to his studies and sport. He studied Arabic, Persian, arithmetic and music, became knowledgeable in the teachings of the Koran, and the craft of the goldsmith. Because he had lived far away from the centre of power, when he ascended the throne in 1520, the Turkish noblemen considered this prince to be mediocre and of little character. Quite soon these views were proven wrong, and two years later the Venetian orator Marco Minio could write that 'he is not a man to let himself be ruled, as had been said'.

Süleyman inaugurated his reign by adopting more liberal measures and abrogating arbitrary laws enacted by his father. He again opened up trade with the East and indemnified merchants who had had their wares confiscated; and he did not increase the customary gift to the Janissaries as was usual on accession to the throne. These initiatives showed, from the start, that the state would be governed with strength and justice, severely but not arbitrarily.

Süleyman perceived power as a synthesis of several component parts and, starting from this premise, he shared the government with a closed circle of men he trusted. His political decisions were coherent, he showed resolve in times of need and, motivated by a strong sense of justice, he succeeded in creating equilibrium in an Empire made up of diverse peoples.

To allow for the needs of such a vast Empire, he introduced substantial changes in legislature and integrated secular laws with Muslim law. A man of action on the field, albeit no warmonger, the Magnificent organized several great campaigns and at the head of his army conquered Rhodes, Iraq, Belgrade, Transylvania, and Hungary. It was only Vienna that he failed to capture. He died on 10 September 1566, far from his beloved Istanbul, on the Hungarian *pushta*, or plain, while attempting to take Szigetvár. Süleyman fascinated his contemporaries, and Western observers recognized his human and political qualities. A patron and lover of the arts, he carried the Crescent to its greatest military victories and to its greatest splendour.

the harem. This was the Kuşhane Kapísí which led through to the Third Court. The two groups of guards were so positioned as to be able to keep close watch at the boundaries between the world outside and the inner palace, beyond which lay the women's quarters.

The Imperial Harem was an institution governed by strict rules. Every person had a precise place assigned according to age and rank. Although wealth, intelligence, ability and not least beauty were here given their due, as indeed they were throughout the rest of Ottoman society, it was a grave fault not to respect the hierarchies, or to be bold, insolent, or discourteous, and the penalties were high.

The seraglio was governed by the sultan's mother, the *valide* sultan, who lodged in apartments in keeping with the importance of her status. Next in rank were the ladies, the *kadïn*, who had borne children to the sultan, and the sultan's favourites, the *ikbal*. Women who were unlikely, or too ugly, to be loved – at any rate by a man – would seek advancement as servants, assuming ever more specialized and important duties.

At the bottom of the social ladder were the novices, girls bought in the many slave markets throughout the Empire or, more often than not, kidnapped by brigands and pirates, who ended up after incredible adventures in the breeding place of the great lord. The career of first lady of the Empire started at this lowest level, and no distinctions of birth, culture, ethnic origin or religion were made. These novices, or *cariye*, lived in the *Cariyeler Dairesi*, near the *Nöbetyeri*, or guards' room. The building was large enough to house a considerable number of people and had, on the ground floor, a small kitchen, the *Cariyeler Mutfaklar*; white marble baths, the *Cariyeler hamamí*; toilets; and a huge laundry, the *Harem Çamaşírlík*. On the first floor were the bedrooms, long dormitories which could accommodate up to a hundred girls, all under rigorous surveillance even at night, with an older woman in charge of each ten girls. Sofas were arranged along the walls leaving a passageway down the centre of the room. These huge dormitories were organized so that they could be easily supervised and at night they were lit by several lamps to 'keep evil at bay and for other needs', as Ottaviano Bon put it.

On the opposite side of the court was the apartment of the princes' nurse, the director of the novices and the chief laundress. The best

Love in the Orient
Venice, Caffè Florian.

THE SULTANA HÜRREM
AN IRON HAND IN A VELVET GLOVE

Hürrem, the wife of Süleyman the Magnificent, played a role of great importance and has not been ignored by observers of the Ottoman world, although judgement upon her has varied. Her origins are not clear, and the fortunes of the young girl have much in common with those of many other girls from the East. She was born in Ruthenia between 1500 and 1506, and may have been called Alexandra Lisowska. She was kidnapped from her home during a Tartar incursion and brought to the palace of the governor of the Crimea, where she was given a good education, and was eventually transferred to the capital. It is not clear whether she began her career in the entourage of the Sultana Hafsa or whether she had been a slave in the harem of Ibrahim Pasha, but certainly one of the two gave her to Süleyman.

The first years in the harem were a hard apprenticeship for the young Russian girl. Being the fourth in line, Hürrem was obliged to submit herself to the will of the sultan's mother and that of the other women, and in particular she was forced to respect the haughty Albanian Gülbahar, who had provided the sultan with the presumed heir to the throne, Prince Mustafa, born in 1515. To the chagrin of her powerful rivals, the young girl made her mark, chiefly due to a playful nature, which prompted Süleyman to give her the name Hürrem, the Happy One, although she was called Roxelana, Roxane or Rosselane, by Europeans on account of her Russian origin. The young girl was soon in the good graces of her lord. Easygoing when this seemed appropriate, seemingly sweet natured but with a strong, unyielding character, she could see far into the human heart and was gifted with intelligence and ambition. The Venetian Ambassador Bernardo Navagero relates this curious episode concerning her rise to favour. Gülbahar, who was the candidate to become the *valide*, upon learning of Hürrem's relations with the sultan, attacked her verbally and physically. A few days later the sultan sent for the Russian girl, but she refused to come into his presence lest her appearance should cause him offence. Full of curiosity, the sultan sent for her again and the girl told him what had taken place. Gülbahar was questioned and confirmed that there had been a quarrel and put forward her reasons. The sultan was displeased by the woman's haughtiness and distanced her from him. Once her powerful rival had been removed from Süleyiman's heart, Hürrem's path was much easier. In about 1530 the sultan overturned an age-old custom, married Hürrem legally and had no further intercourse with other women. Ten years later she was assisted by another stroke of luck: because of a fire in the old seraglio, Hürrem moved into the Topkapí Palace.

Hürrem was brutal and determined in the use of power. In Istanbul her name is recorded in the lovely baths she built facing the basilica of Hagia Sophia. She died in 1558 and was buried on the Third Hill of Constantinople in a small mausoleum in Süleyman's lovely mosque, surrounded by roses.

Imaginary scenes from the harem
recreated by Princess Hatice's favourite
architect, Ignaz Mellin.
Ignaz Mellin, *Voyage pittoresque de
Constantinople et du Bosphore*, Paris, 1819.
Parma, Biblioteca Palatina.

room was the finely panelled nurse's room, divided by a vast armoire and furnished with wall cupboards. It had a spacious balcony which the nurse and her charges could enjoy in good weather or when the sun shone. There was a magnificent view from this balcony, since it overlooked the gardens, and the distant view was of the Bosporus and the Sea of Marmara. A flight of stairs next to this room led down to the gardens below.

Another entrance led to the harem hospital, the *Cariyeler Hastanesi*. It was reached by a long flight of stone steps, punctuated by small landings, which gave access to rooms on either side. In the centre of the building was a courtyard, surrounded by a double portico with eight columns, which was planted with trees and cool in the summer. The atmosphere was romantic and alluring even though it was a place for the sick. Today the rooms, all of different sizes, are in a precarious state of repair. All the necessary facilities were here: a huge bath with a wonderful marble fountain, rooms on two floors for the kitchen staff, and the kitchen itself was a very high room on the ground floor which could cater for at least fifty people. Next door were the toilets, and on the same side of the courtyard were various other rooms that were probably furnished as day rooms rather than hospital wards. However, there is doubt about what their function actually was: it seems rather incongruous that the hospital should be larger than the quarters of the novices for whom it was intended. Such a vast and well set-out complex suggests a place suitable for a bustling throng of people, a place in constant use, rather than a sick bay where the number of people would constantly vary.

If up to now this description of the House of Felicity sems to

Drinking vessels decorated with precious stones. The sultans' many domestic objects were often so profusely covered in diamonds, rubies and emeralds that the shape of the original was obliterated. These decorations were intended to produce a chromatic effect, rather than precision in the detail.
Istanbul, Topkapí.

be of a kind of convent inhabited by eunuchs and cloistered virgins, there was also a more intimate and secret area where life went on with a more voluptuous rhythm. This was the part reserved for the sultan's beloved and it communicated with the *mâbeyin*, the ruler's apartment, through a long corridor decorated with fine ceramics and known as the *Altïnyol*, the Golden Way.

Intimacy with 'the most absolute monarch on Earth' could be measured by the degree of physical proximity, and the imperial women most favoured by love, fortune and respect were the mother, wives and favourites of the reigning sultan. Starting at the lowest level, the favourites probably occupied part of the tall three-storied building next to the guardroom. The women who attended the sultan lived separately from the novices.

At the centre lived the sultan's mother, 'the pearl of the Caliphate', respected and loved throughout the Empire. The *valide*'s apartment consisted of four rooms facing on to a square courtyard. There was a waiting room, or *sofa*, on the right, elegantly decorated and furnished. A passage led to two other rooms: the dining room or *Yemek Odasi*, adorned with wonderful tiles, a beautiful marble fountain and huge cupboards with doors inlaid with mother-of-pearl. The bedroom was equally elegant, furnished with a low divan which, Turkish fashion, could be used during the day for sitting and at night for sleeping. The ceramic tiles on the walls contained designs of vases, from which trees grew, with a background of delicate turquoise. The colour of the sea seen on the walls was a reflection of the sea beyond the terrace of the apartment of the sultana, who could gaze on the Bosporus from the shelter of a golden canopy.

The apartment was sited so as to control the whole seraglio. This was the *valide*'s job, since she held the same office in the harem as that held by the sultan in the Topkapí. She administered a whole government in miniature, made up of ministers, officials and attendants, all female, except for the eunuchs. The sultan could enter the harem through the room that held the harem treasure and so go to the apartments of the four most important women.

The size of the rooms of the first lady of the Empire, known as *başkadin*, was proportionate to her high rank. Only the woman who produced the first male heir, the future successor to the Ottoman throne, was given this title. She had noble and refined rooms, a court of her own and an income sufficiently large to allow her to give and spend with largesse. All the members of the seraglio formally recognized her role as first lady and were obliged to pay her appropriate respect and reverence.

The living quarters of the other wives led off from her rooms. They too had special privileges; their own apartments, a court and servants, richly elegant gowns and jewellery, and they enjoyed an income adequate to their rank of second, third or fourth wife.

The sultan's heirs also lived in the House of Felicity, looked after by healthy and expert nurses. The sons of the same

Wet-nurses employed to suckle the royal infants came from healthy and hardy peasant families. At the conclusion of their period of service they were generously rewarded.
Costumi orientali, XVII century, Bologna, Biblioteca Comunale dell'Archiginnasio.

mother were brought up together; those of different mothers were brought up separately on account of the jealousy which existed among the heirs to the throne. From the age of five the boys had a tutor, the *hoca*, who came daily to the harem to give them their first lessons. The tutor was closely watched by the black eunuchs and had no opportunity of seeing the women. Once circumcised, at about eleven years of age, the princes were separated from their mothers and given quarters outside the seraglio in the company of their tutors. The education of these youths took place far away from the capital. They were given official appointments in the provinces of the Empire, where each established himself with his mother and his own court.

The life of the sultan's daughters was very different. They were not involved in the rivalries and jealousies that were part of the boys' existence. Free from diffidence and suspicion, the princesses were loved unconditionally. Ottoman history has many instances of rivalry between a sultan and his sons, rivalries which frequently ended in murder provoked by the least suspicion of rebellion or betrayal. In contrast, the sultan's attitude to his daughters was often one of sincere and profound affection, unsullied by any calculating doubts. Many of the princesses enjoyed enormous power, great freedom of movement and also vast wealth.

The sovereign's aunts and sisters were also part of that small privileged group. They were served by a host of slaves, dressed lavishly and lived in the seraglio until they married. It was the Ottoman custom that they should marry the highest officials in the land, and to this end the sultan was obliged to provide them with a dowry which allowed them to maintain, even outside the palace, a lifestyle commensurate with their royal rank.

As its name implies, the harem was an inviolable place, 'closed and reserved'. The women's quarters – and this is true of even the most humble Muslim household – were a refuge that no profane glance might violate. Lady Wortley Montagu reports in astonishment that even the master of the house would adopt an attitude of respect on entering the harem, and should he by chance see in front of the door an unfamiliar ladies' shoe, he would not hesitate to withdraw at once. It was the Turkish custom to show such respect towards a place that was to them

At the Ottoman court objects of Western technology, such as clocks and telescopes, became collectors' items. Istanbul, Topkapí.

Decorative ceramic tiles in the
apartment of the sultana mother.
Ornamental ceramic murals, much used
in Turkey to decorate pavilions and
mosques, were an integral part of the
architectural design, creating a most
effective homogenous effect.
Istanbul, Topkapí.

almost sacred, and even the crudest men took care not to violate the sanctum. This Ottoman harem as an institution has again and again been singled out by Europeans as a stage for untold delights or unspeakable hell, as a woman's undisputed domain or as her prison, as a scene from *The Thousand and One Nights* or a place of mystery, intrigue and silence.

For a Roxelana, enamoured of power, or even for a Cecilia Baffo-Venier, who preferred a life with the sultan to the drab existence of an illegitimate girl living under the severe rule of the Republic of Venice, the harem would have provided a throne from which to engage on an equal footing with the men in power at the time. For those delicate and well-nourished young girls, walking silently through the gardens of the seraglio beside their mighty Ottoman lord, the harem must have seemed a far more comfortable place than the villages they came from, where misery was all-pervading and where their fate would have certainly been much

NUR BANU
A EUROPEAN WOMAN ON THE THRONE OF ISTANBUL

Nur Banu was the wife of Selim II. She was either of Cypriot or Venetian origin, and has been often confused with another powerful woman. Scholars put forward conflicting hypotheses about her identity. Some think she was a Cypriot called Kalè Kartánou, and that she was born in about 1530 and kidnapped from her family. Others believe her to have been Cecilia Baffo-Venier, a Venetian patrician who had been kidnapped in 1537 by Barabarossa on the island of Paros, in the Venetian–Turkish war. According to this version, Cecilia was born in 1525, the daughter of Nicolo Venier, Lord of Paros, and of the lady Violante Baffo. The marriage was not registered in Venice, perhaps because it was not legitimate.

The girl, now a slave, was taken to Constantinople. Elegant and distinguished, she was brought into the seraglio of Prince Selim and given the name of Nur Banu, Lady Light, an indication of her beauty. The years she spent with the Turk cannot have been pleasant. Selim was not an attractive person. Lustful and so fat that he could not sit on a horse, he drank to excess. But Nur used her intelligence to establish herself, and in 1546 their union was cemented by the birth of Prince Murat.

In 1559 a certain Hasan appeared in Venice, purporting to have been sent by Selim to gather information about the family of the princess. The Senate confirmed the Venetian origin of the lady and furnished information on her family, but these preliminary meetings were marred by the suspicion that the man was an impostor. The Senate investigated, but fruitlessly. This matter of great delicacy was complicated by the fact that Nur and Selim were living in a distant province of the Empire.

The quality of Cecilia's character became even more evident when Selim became sultan, but it was really only fully revealed in the reign of Murat. Mother and son were very close. Nur loved to emphasize her role as mother in the ritual formulae that were appended to her name; for his part, Murat, who was skilful in matters of state, allowed the *valide* immense authority. The sultana took a hand in the Empire's affairs: she proposed ministers; kept in contact with Europe, in particular with Venice; and carried on a correspondence with other such important women as Catherine de' Medici.

Nur became the perfect embodiment of Ottoman culture, and if in private she maintained European habits, in public she gave no sign of them. She visited Muslim saints, made her devotions and used her wealth to promote charitable works. She died suddenly on 7 December 1583 after a shattering illness. There was a suspicion of poisoning, at the instigation of Murat's wife Safiye, who for years had been openly hostile to the *valide*. According to her wishes, the sultana was buried within the complex of Hagia Sophia in a magnificently decorated mausoleum. Perhaps her last wish expressed her desire to join together once more the broken thread of her Christian and European origins.

The placid rhythm of the day encouraged idleness and laziness and passing time with wandering around the gardens: a life free from pressure and filled with voluptuousness in the best tradition of the Orient.
Costumi orientali, XVII century, Bologna, Biblioteca Comunale dell'Archiginnasio.

worse. For those women who were prey to secret vices and evil thoughts, and ran into trouble or transgressed the rules, the harem became 'a slope which juts out from the walls leading to the sea below. It is from that place, they say, that those faithless odalisques who have displeased their master for any reason are slid into the Bosporus, stuffed in a sack with a cat and a snake. How many marvellous bodies have the swift currents of those deep blue waters culled!'

Turks from different social classes in front of the Imperial Gate at the Topkapí.
Antonio Baratta, *Costantinopoli effigiata e descritta*, Torino, 1840. Venice, Biblioteca Nazionale Marciana.

SLAVES, ODALISQUES, AND SULTANAS

His favourites delighted the great lord
with music. The Turks took this type of
entertainment from the refined
customs of the Byzantine court, and
over the years many of the sultans
became accomplished musicians
and performers.
Codice Cicogna, *Memorie turchesche*,
XVII century. Venice, Biblioteca del
Museo Correr.

The Turks had led an extraordinary life, full of adventure, in the steppes of Central Asia. The pleasures of galloping on horses, raping girls, getting drunk, shedding blood and other acts of violence were mingled with feelings of tolerance and brotherhood. They delighted in games of dice, in aliossi, riddles and long stories and also in hunting (a surrogate for war), in drinking and in lovemaking. It was, indeed, the love of women rather than of riches which spurred these nomads into action, for – as Gengis Khan crudely put it – there is no madder joy that of clasping to one's own bosom the wives and the daughters of one's enemies.

In a world where even games were violent, women enjoyed both consideration and freedom. Even when a woman was seen as prey, her conquest had for these men the same meaning as that of war or of the hunt. Games, tournaments, competitions were the rituals which accompanied mating. A girl would mount her horse, slinging a ram across her saddle, and her suitors would give chase. He who managed to seize the beast married the girl. Free huntresses and warriors, these women had precise duties, carried responsibility within the tribe, and their role was important in the sparse nomadic habitat.

With the adoption of the Islamic religion and a strict moral code, Turkish society and the place of women within it changed, and their autonomy was limited. Among the lower classes monogamy still prevailed, but at higher levels the harem was adopted. In Arabic *haramgah*, *zanana*, *harim* signify a 'closed place, sacred, reserved'; its Persian counterpart is *enderun* and the Indian, *purdah* or *zenana*. All words designate that part of the house reserved for the women. In Turkish it was at first given the poetic name of *dârüssaâde*, the House of Felicity, and later that of harem, a word more frequently adopted and the one most used in the West.

The famous harem of the Ottoman sultans, renowned for its size, splendour and elegance, was called the *Harem-i-Hümayun*, the Imperial Harem. The whole history and gradual decay of this institution is closely linked to the rule of the Crescent,

The opulent metropolis of Constantinople provides the background for this portrait of an elegantly attired Greek lady.
George De La Chappelle, *Recuel de divers portraits*, Paris 1648. Venice, Biblioteca Nazionale Marciana.

PORTRAITS: THE GREEK GIRL

She was seated at the far end of a divan, a young, blonde, Greek girl with the well-known profile of the ancient statues. A *taktikos* from Smyrna, with scalloped edges and golden buttons, sat flirtatiously over one ear. Her hair was bound into two enormous braids wound like a turban around her head, which admirably complemented the spiritual quality of her face. A sparkling intelligence in her blue eyes lit up her face, in direct contrast with the still and vacant brilliance in the great black eyes of her beautiful rivals.

De Nerval, *Voyage en Orient*, 1884

which also underlines its expansion. The harem became a myth for all Europeans, who saw it above all as a place of pleasure, but it was primarily a formidable centre of power where important political decisions were often taken. It may have given the appearance of a city utterly separated from Constantinople, but its involvement with the interests and passions of the Turkish world and beyond were quite extraordinary.

The hierarchy of the Imperial Harem was identical to that of the Topkapí, and with a few exceptions the function assigned to each woman had its equivalent in the male world. The place of each was established by very precise regulations and every lady had her duties and her privileges. The women of the seraglio were the slaves of the Sublime Porte and not always ethnic Turks. Only the early sultans married women of their own race or, for political expediency, took Christian princesses in marriage. Sultan Orhan, who lived between the thirteenth and the fourteenth centuries, took Nilüfer, the daughter of a Greek prince, as his bride, and later Theodora, the daughter of the Byzantine emperor John VI Cantacuzenus.

However, the custom of marriage soon fell into disuse. In the Ottoman world, ethnic origin was of little importance and there was no policy for establishing the supremacy of the Turkish race. The custom of importing slaves into the palace was adopted in order to avoid factions and rebellions, since they had been uprooted from their native lands and had virtually no family ties.

Women for the Imperial Harem were usually recruited in the same way. Provincial governors, pashas and other imperial dignitaries who wished to pay tribute to their sovereign would send young slaves to the seraglio as gifts. And during the *Kurban Bayramí*, the Islamic Feast of the Sacrifice, members of the royal family made the sultan a present of a slave girl. These girls had to be particularly endowed with beauty and grace, but were also expected to have a good education and refined tastes. They were carefully trained for eight or nine years and taught to sing, make music and dance, until ready to be presented at the palace.

Most of them were Tartars, Circassians and Georgians, all thought to be among the most beautiful races in the world. But there were also several European girls who

Courtesan.
Michel Baudier, *L'Histoire de la decadence de l'empire grec*, Paris, 1650. Venice, Biblioteca Nazionale Marciana.

PORTRAITS: THE CIRCASSIAN GIRL

The girl in the middle of the divan was a Circassian, as was obvious from the huge black eyes that contrasted with a milky white complexion. Other clear signs of her race were her aquiline nose, which had a pure and elegant shape, her rather long neck, her tall and slim build and her delicate hands and feet.

On her head she wore a gold-flecked turban from which escaped a profusion of jet-black tresses which enhanced her rouge-tinged cheeks. She wore a jacket embroidered with little scenes and edged with frills and silk scallops. The many-coloured strands formed a cordon of flowers at the edge of the material. A silver belt and wide trousers made of pink lamé silk completed her attire, which was both elegant and charming.

As is the custom, her eyes were made up with *surme* in order to enlarge and enliven them. Her long nails and the palms of her hands had been tinted orange by henna, as were her bare feet. These she daintily curled up on the divan and made the silver rings around her ankles tinkle from time to time.

De Nerval, *Voyage en Orient*, 1884

had been kidnapped by pirates and sold to rich Ottoman masters. A few came from the slave markets, but usually girls recruited in this way were imported into the harem as servants, and given menial tasks to perform. Wherever they came from, whether as a gift or purchased in a slave market, once they reached the court they were examined by the eunuchs, and if they had the smallest physical defect or blemish, were rejected. The ones who were accepted were taken to the queen mother for her approval.

Slave girls could improve their position and move up in the hierarchy, but the way was difficult and full of snares, enemies and traps. These *cariye,* or slaves, had first to make a profession of faith and become Muslim. In order to adore the merciful and exclusive God of Islam it was enough to recite, in the presence of two witnesses, the *şehadet,* a simple formula that runs thus: 'Allah is great, and Mohammed is His Prophet'. Slave girls provided the only cases of forced conversion that was practised by the Turks. It was much more usual for Europeans to renounce the Christian faith voluntarily and convert to Islam for idealistic or opportunistic reasons, in order to avoid a sentence, for example, or to further a career. The girls were given a new name, often Persian, something sweet and suggestive such as Safay, 'Pleasing One'; Perestû, 'Little Swallow'; Gülbahar, 'Rose of Spring'; Mahpeyker, 'Moon-shaped one'; Şekerbuli, 'Sugar Crystal'; Dilbeste, 'She who Enamours the Heart'; or Nilüfer Nenufaro, 'Lotus of the Yellow Flowers', strong as the sorbet which is made from its sweetness. The names tended to reflect the girls' characters or particular attributes.

The teachers in charge of the education of these girls followed their instruction with meticulous care. They were taught to read and write in Ottoman, to sew and to embroider, and if they had any special aptitude for it they were trained in singing, music and dance. They lived under the strict supervision of the teachers and older inmates; time was marked by precise duties and the monotony of each day was broken only by a few hours of recreation or a special outing. European travellers were quite right when they used the analogy of the seminary to describe the seraglio, because there was little difference between the two. The slave girls were governed by a rigid discipline, and any infringement of the rules was severely punished.

The life of the harem, like the rest of the Topkapí, was organized into several services called *oda* through which a complex court life was managed. The slaves in the harem

were assigned to a particular service and remained there until they had learned a particular skill. They could move up in their field or pass into another, according to their individual talent, resolve and intelligence. Their future was decided during this apprenticeship. The most beautiful and sensual girls, those outstandingly graceful and with ability, were sent to the court of the sovereign's mother or those of his wives and were then in a position to be noticed and to become a favourite. The less lucky women, those who were not chosen to be loved by the sultan, could make careers as skilled servants or governesses, and so enjoy appreciable status.

The harem was the woman's empire, governed by the the *valide* sultan, the queen mother, in conjunction with a close circle of ministers who formed her cabinet. The *kethüda*, a kind of general overseer in charge of the running of the various departments and responsible for the efficient performance of the staff, held the place of prime minister. When she was installed, the governor received from the sultan the official seal, a jewel and a robe embroidered in silver to be used on state occasions. The symbol of her office was a silver mace.

Under her was the *hazinedar usta,* or chief treasurer, who held a very responsible administrative position. The harem budget was considerable, and she administered the payment of salaries, current expenses and pensions to the elderly when they left the seraglio.

The women in charge of the various services were called *usta*, a term literally signifying teacher, which was used here for the women in charge of the servants and the slaves. The *çamaşir usta* ran the laundry and cared for the imperial robes.

Slavery was widespread in the Ottoman world, despite the Islamic deprecation of it. In the capital there were many slave markets.
Costumi orientali, XVII century. Bologna, Biblioteca Comunale dell'Archiginnasio.

There was a special ceremonial routine for the washing of the sultan's clothes, and the basins and clothes lines, always of silver, were kept exclusively for the imperial wardrobe.

A somewhat risky job was that of chief taster. At a time when court intrigues were daily events, the life of a prince was very precarious. This woman's task was to taste the food of the sultan and make sure that it had not been poisoned. She assisted at each meal, standing beside him, to make sure that the service was impeccable. Attired with great care, she wore wide red *şalvar* (trousers) and a long gown enlivened by a yellow handkerchief.

Traditionally, Turks placed great importance in the use of the bath. In the West this custom was lost because the Christian attitude of prudery led to despising the body. But in the East, partly due to Koranic precepts of ritual cleansing, bathing was carried out with great care. The *ibriktar usta*, or superintendent of the baths, therefore enjoyed an important function. The *hamam* was a place where the sultan often came to relax and gossip. Since Turkish saunas were temperate, whole days might be spent in them. The supervisor, with the help of her assistants, reigned over this little world. She provided the pitchers, soap, unguents and towels. The *berber usta* shaved the sultan and directed a group of girl barbers.

The lords of the Bosporus were considered barbarians by Western observers, but they followed a very complex ceremonial at court which they had inherited from Byzantium. Daily rituals became solemn practices, made all the more imposing by the luxury which they found so necessary, as well as by the vast number of servants executing these ceremonies. One of these related to coffee. In charge of this ritual was the *kahveci usta*, or coffee steward, who supervised this service and the girls of the *oda* who served the beverage. Five concubines brought the coffee to the

PORTRAITS: THE ARMENIAN GIRL

Next was a girl from Armenia whose costume, less richly barbarian, was closer to the contemporary fashion in Constantinople. A fez, like those worn by the men, covered in a thick cloud of blue silk knotted together and tied back, adorned her head. Her profile was slightly arched and held a fierce expression, but her serenity was almost like that of an animal. Her green velvet bodice was decorated with a wide border of swans' down, whose sparkling whiteness enhanced the elegance of her neck. Around this she wore thin chains with silver pendant aigrettes. Her waist was encircled in golden plates embossed with big filigree buttons and, with a totally modern touch, on her feet, from which she had cast off her *babouche* on to the carpet, she wore silk stockings with occasional embroidery.

De Nerval, *Voyage en Orient*, 1884

Women paid a high price in order to become the favourites of the sultan, or first ladies of the Empire. If they transgressed the strict rules of the harem they were severely punished.
Costumi orientali, XVII century. Bologna, Biblioteca Comunale dell'Archiginnasio.

Turkish woman intent on her weaving. *Raccolta di 120 stampe*, Venetiis, 1783. Venice, Biblioteca Nazionale Marciana.

facing page
Everyday activities of the Turks in Constantinople: gossip and relaxation in the baths; *below*, animated dealings in the slave market.
Antonio Baratta, *Costantinopoli effigiata e descritta*, Torino, 1840. Venice, Biblioteca Nazionale Marciana.

sultan and his guests. One carried the gold and silver tray on which the cups were arranged. Two held the silk tablecloth embroidered with pearls, another carried the *cevze*, a small pot used in the preparation of Turkish coffee, and the last served the beverage. The ceremony took place frequently, always under the watchful eyes of the steward. Turks would drink this celebrated 'black beverage' several times a day, and soon it was to conquer the tables of all Europe.

An enormous quantity of food was consumed in the harem: languorously reclining on their divans, the women would continuously eat sweets and cakes while engaged in some pastime or conversation. The *kilerci usta* looked after the pantry, which at all times had to be fully stocked with rare and costly food and drink. The odalisques who belonged to the *oda* would bring to the table fruit, cakes and sorbets, of which the Turks were very fond. At the court of Istanbul etiquette was observed with great care, almost punctiliously, and was a means for rigidly maintaining proper distance and hierarchy. The *saray usta*, or mistress of ceremonies, oversaw all births, weddings, circumcisions, official and religious celebrations, and she had to be conversant with the rank and the precedence of each person. She presided over every ceremony and instructed everybody in the behaviour they should adopt in the presence of the sultan and the imperial family. Her authority, and the power she wielded were symbolized by a silver baton and a seal that she bore.

The *baskâtibe*, or first secretary, was responsible for discipline and conduct, and had various assistants. She also controlled the *kalfa*, the older serving women. The odalisques were overseen by the *vekil usta*, the female prefect, who had her apartment in the quarter reserved for the slaves, from whose ranks she had risen. Her chief task was training the girls.

The role of the *kutucu usta*, the personal servants of the *valide* sultan and the wives was important. Their task was to give competent and skilful assistance to their mistresses at the baths, and assist them with their wardrobe and hair. In the late Ottoman period, when the harem became excessively vast, and expenses rocketed, each princess had more than one private maid. These servants, in continual intimacy with their mistresses, often became very influential.

In the Ottoman world women had considerable power: they were familiar with herbs and unguents; used such paediatric medical practices, unknown in Europe, as vaccination; saw to pregnancies and childbirth, the exclusive province of women; and they performed skilfully a form of medicine different from that used by men, that was to be found in books which they often ignored. Only in very

rare cases did they have recourse to doctors from outside. Their health care was in the hands of the *hastalar usta,* or chief nurse, and her assistants. Even the sultans respected the midwives and the wet-nurses, known as *sütnine,* or milk mothers. Nannies and wet-nurses were chosen from highly respectable families outside the palace circles, and as guardians of the young princes they enjoyed a prestigious position. Lastly there was the *musahip kadin,* who was in the personal service of the sultan and whose duties corresponded to those of the white eunuchs in the men's household.

The slaves and servants received a daily salary in silver coins which varied according to their jobs and which was paid punctually every three months. Over and above their salaries, the women were given their clothing, consisting of two cloth dresses per year, a silk dress, a piece of pale material for shirts and a lighter one for handkerchiefs. What they received depended, of course, on the taste and generosity of the *valide* and the sultan, who could at their pleasure hand out additional gifts to their servants.

These women were not lifetime slaves. They were obliged to remain at court for nine years only, and after this could leave and get married should they wish. In this event, they received a certificate of enfranchisement and could collect the money they had saved during their years of service. To this was added the presents they

Important dignitaries and members of the royal family gave slave girls as gifts to the sultan. The girls had to be endowed with beauty and grace, be well educated and have good taste. Before they were presented at court they received a thorough education. *Costumi orientali*, XVII century. Bologna, Biblioteca Comunale dell'Archiginnasio.

received from their friends and from the *valide*, and if they retired after a longer period of service they were given homes and land. The amounts received were considerable and often these servants were able to set themselves up most satisfactorily. Freed slaves received many proposals of marriage and could choose from among their suitors. Because of their substantial dowries and connections with their former mistresses, these women could act as valuable intermediaries for their husbands and as a consequence could make the fortunes of the families into which they married.

A page serves the coffee, the celebrated 'black drink' that the lands of the Crescent made known throughout Europe.
Foggie diverse del vestire de' Turchi, XV century. Venice, Biblioteca Nazionale Marciana.

Many of the women in the Imperial Harem were Tartars, Circassian and Georgian, but there were also many European girls, kidnapped by pirates and sold to rich Ottoman buyers.
Costumi orientali, XVII century. Bologna, Biblioteca Comunale dell'Archiginnasio.

THE LONG CAREER OF THE FIRST LADY OF THE EMPIRE

The little Circassian girl Tirimûjân was dancing with graceful gestures before the sultan Abdül Mecit, who showed his approval by the intensity with which he watched her. It was the time of *Kurban Bayramí*, the Feast of the Sacrifice, and the twenty-year-old sultan was visiting his newly married fourteen-year-old sister in her lovely wooden house on the Bosporus. Seeing her brother's interest, the princess thought to please him by making him a present of the girl, and it was thus that the mountain lass from the Caucasus ended up at the Topkapí.

Keen and very ambitious, Tirimûjân soon learned the lessons the eunuchs and the *kalfas* had to teach. She perfected her techniques in the art of lovemaking and found favour with the sultan. Step by step she climbed the slippery ladder to power and eventually gave birth to a son, Abdul Hamit II. He eventually mounted the Osmanli throne and was known by the fierce nickname of 'The Red Sultan'. At this moment, the first half of the nineteenth century, life smiled on the little dancer, but she did not see her son mount the throne since she died very young, struck down by consumption.

Tirimûjân's fate showed the path women had to tread in order to become the wife of the greatest monarch of the universe. Beauty, intelligence and a lot of luck were necessary ingredients for success, and it was not easy to keep these for many years. The girls upon whom the master's glance had rested were called *gedikli*. All that was needed was for the sultan to make some trite observation or show a tiny bit of interest and a girl's life changed completely.

If the sultan indicated a desire to spend the night with a girl, she was ritually prepared. She was washed, massaged, perfumed, and dressed in fine linen and sumptuous robes, her hair was dressed, she was covered in jewels, and thus attired she was taken to the great lord. On the following morning, after the night of love, the sultan would give her a present commensurate with the degree of satisfaction she had given him. If it was a new passion and not simply a concubine who had already been in the master's bed, the talk of the harem the next day would be of nothing else and the gossip would be accompanied by malicious smiles.

On entering the harem the girls professed the Muslim faith and were given a new name. Then, under the guidance of teachers and eunuchs, they continued their apprenticeship.
Costumi orientali, XVII century. Bologna, Biblioteca Comunale dell'Archiginnasio.

Moving up the first step of the hierarchy the girls became favourites (*ikbal*), and were separated from the common slaves. The sultan, as absolute master of his harem, could choose a different woman every night or could continue for a long time with one or another according to the pleasure he received and the interest that the girl managed to keep alive. The favourites were treated with respect by the servants and eunuchs. Ottoman history records some sober sovereigns who were less inclined to pleasure but also some very lustful sultans who had ten or so concubines and a vast army of children.

The favourite who gave birth to a son became a *kadín* and was recognized as an official wife. Like any other Muslim, the sultan could have four wives and order was rigorously established according to the birth of sons. The mother of the first-born son and presumed heir to the throne was called *başkadín,* or first lady. Then there were second, third and fourth wives. If a son died, the mother lost all her prerogatives and gave up her place to the woman who, after her, had given birth to another heir.

During the first Ottoman era the wives of the great lord were given the title of *hatun* and then *kadín* or *kadín efendi*, corresponding to the title of lady. From the sixteenth century onwards, they were called *haseki sultan*. The wives lived surrounded by every comfort in separate apartments and could count on huge incomes which they often used to build hospitals, public baths, fountains, kitchens for the poor or mosques. In the lands of the Crescent, the sultan and ruling classes were entrusted with the erection of public buildings. This was both a right and duty to which the first ladies of the Sublime Porte made a considerable contribution. The princesses attached their names to these architectural works and in each century contributed to the embellishment of the country.

The *kadín* did not love one other yet spent time together observing the customs imposed by the rigid court etiquette, which decreed the exchange of visits and presents at childbirth and religious events. Despite the titles given to them and

ABDÜL HAMIT II, 'THE RED SULTAN'

Abdül Hamit came to the throne on 3 August 1876 with all the immutable solemnity of Ottoman etiquette: an oath of loyalty, the girding of the sword in the Eyüp Mosque, reviewing of the troops and a reception for dignitaries and ministers. Seated on a white horse, His Highness processed through the streets of Constantinople wearing on his head a fez undecorated by any diamond and dressed in sober robes, which only emphasized the magnificence of those worn by the imperial functionaries.

The young sultan, despite his fabulous and hieratic inheritance, had not received much preparation for his position nor been given much information about his vast empire, which encompassed an explosive mixture of diverse peoples, all with particular needs. In his youth Abdül Hamit had been a keen student, interested in mathematics and eager to learn history, but these inclinations were curtailed by a mediocre education at court. He was timid and introverted, lonely and not much loved by his father, who preferred the brilliant Murat. Unable to arouse interest and sympathy in others, he spent a lonely childhood, attracted only to people with complex personalities like his own. He was brought to power by the progressive movement and soon showed himself to be an autocrat and a conservative. His habit of spying, which had made his brothers loathe him as a child, now became the state practice as secret accusations were encouraged.

At court he insisted on formal appearances and behaviour, but in his private life he appreciated an independent opinion or a witty and salacious joke. In public he displayed great religious fervour and imposed the strict observance of religious duties, but again, in private, he demonstrated a keen critical sense and considerable scepticism concerning the supernatural.

In many ways Abdül Hamit was an actor, who played his part perfectly, when this seemed opportune and appealing to him. As sultan and caliph he encouraged and propagated the union of all Muslims in order to combat the breaking up of the Empire. For this reason his rule was dominated by religious fanaticism and racial strife, and antagonism between the various ethnic groups.

Called 'The Red Sultan' on account of the blood that flowed during his reign, he attempted some demagogic reforms, built schools and hospitals and sought to improve transportation. But these were done to help the people and not to modernize the country. Abdül Hamit was a ruler dominated by fear, and his life seemed punctuated by deeds which misfired and desires which were repressed or unexpressed. He spent his life uncovering plots and attempts on his life, but this did not save him from deposition and melancholy exile, which he passed at Salonika, along with three *kadín*, two princes, four eunuchs and fourteen servants, an entourage far too modest for a man who had believed himself invincible.

An attendant combs the hair of a young lady in the baths. Not all the women at the palace became favourites, and those who were not successful could make a career as a specialized servant and attain some wealth and status.
Raccolta di 120 stampe, Venetiis, 1783. Venice, Biblioteca Nazionale Marciana.

facing page
An Ottoman sultana with her slave. The harem servants received a daily wage and after nine years could leave their service and get married. Freed women received many proposals of marriage since their considerable dowry and their relationship with their former mistresses would benefit the family into which they married.
Raccolta di 120 stampe, Venetiis, 1783. Venice, Biblioteca Nazionale Marciana.

the favourable conditions they enjoyed, these women were not legally married. Matrimony was exceptional since it was perceived almost as a weakness and was harshly criticized by prominent Turks. However all the children were considered legitimate, a general principle that was in force throughout the whole Ottoman Empire, where no distinction was made between children born from concubines and those from wives.

The fate of the *haseki sultan* was closely linked to that of her lord. At the death of a sultan his wives and favourites were transferred to the old seraglio and only the mother of the new heir, together with her court, remained at the Topkapí. The older women, the sick and those in disgrace ended up in the Palace of Tears, as the residence on the Third Hill was sadly called. The place had a sinister reputation and brought to mind distancing and decadence. There was however a custom that at the death of the sovereign his women could remarry. With the consent of the new lord, they married men of medium to high rank, and frequently these unions were influenced by relationships the ladies managed to form with those newly in power, as well as by the riches they had managed to accumulate over time.

To achieve real power it was not sufficient merely to remain in the monarch's favour: it was necessary to give him a son and to fight to place this son on the throne. Such high stakes created savage competition between the wives in the harem. Factions were formed in which servants, eunuchs and high dignitaries were aligned. The ladies fought each other, at times even coming to blows, and used any form of treachery in order to promote their own sons. In the classic era, power was in the hands of strong and capable sultans, but with the decline of the Empire, corruption and manipulation of the system came more and more uncontrollable palace feuds, which cost many women their lives.

preceding pages
Jules Migonney, *The Moorish
Bath*, 1911. Bourg-en-Bresse,
Musée de Brou.

The royal princesses married
only noblemen and Ottoman
dignitaries, not foreign
princes. They had rich dowries
and kept their considerable
court endowment so that
even as married women they
could maintain the superb
lifestyle to which they were
accustomed.
Costumi orientali, XVII century.
Bologna, Biblioteca Comunale
dell'Archiginnasio.

DAGGERS DRAWN
THE ROYAL PRINCESSES

The birth of a male child was announced with salvoes of cannon; rejoicing among the people; processions of dignitaries who came from the most distant provinces to pay homage; and letters of congratulation from foreign potentates brought with great pomp by dignified ambassadors. The birth of a female child was greeted with far less formality and enthusiasm.

Throughout their infancy, children of the sultan, whether they be boys or girls, lived with their mothers, but from birth they were treated differently according to their sex. Several eunuchs and a tutor looked after the boys and gave them their first lessons in archery, hunting, physical exercise, horsemanship and the use of arms. The princes were also taught a craft. In the East there was no dichotomy, such as existed in Europe, between manual and intellectual labour. On the contrary, an education was considered complete only when both were mastered.

After their circumcision, the young princes acquired a greater degree of autonomy. Often their father sent them to one of the provinces, where they took up a government position. They were accompanied by their tutor, their mother, courtiers, artists and men of letters, so bringing to the cities where they set up their courts the culture of the capital, and reproducing in miniature the court of Istanbul. They encouraged the arts, literature, the building of monuments and of the infrastructure. It was customary for the princes to be sent to Asian rather than European provinces in order to keep them away from the snares of Christian princes and their habits, which might lead them astray.

The path that the princesses followed was totally different: they lived at court until they married, and were much loved by their fathers because the relationship was not poisoned by suspicion and rivalry. Less care was taken with their education than with that given to the boys. They did, however, learn to read and write, as well as those skills deemed necessary and considered more suitable for a woman's education, such as singing, music and embroidery.

Aunts, sisters and daughters of the sultan never allied themselves to foreign princes, but married only high-ranking dignitaries of the Ottoman court. At the time of their marriage, the sultan gave them a rich dowry of property, gold, jewels and an expensive wardrobe. When they married, princesses did not relinquish the royal dowry that was theirs while they resided within the palace, and took with them to their new homes their favourite eunuchs and slaves, whose salaries were paid for by the sultan. It was necessary for these royal ladies once they married to maintain the same lifestyle they had enjoyed at court, and as a consequence the bride-groom had to be a leisured and wealthy person; he would derive great advantage from the union, since the sultan would offer him high office and privileges.

The marriage of a princess was celebrated for days. Once the marriage contract, in which the dowry was agreed, had been drawn up, the groom sent out invitations to the most important people in the state. The bride's ornaments would be transported to the seraglio: they consisted of rings, earrings, buckles, mirrors, high slippers for the bath and other objects decorated with precious stones and pearls. Silver platters arrived, stacked high with cakes, and a gold diadem set with precious stones, a Byzantine custom which the Turks continued. The bride's trousseau was displayed in a room where the important dignitaries of the Empire came to leave their gifts, and was then taken with great pomp to the princess's new home.

The day after the ceremony, the high officials of the court and the royal ladies accompanied the bride to her new home, where she was received by her husband and the head of the black eunuchs. They escorted her to the door of her harem, supporting her under the arms. Splendid banquets, one for the men, another for the women, were laid out. As the guests departed, they were offered a gift by the

The luxurious residence of a royal princess situated in the Eyüp quarter in Constantinople.
Antonio Baratta, *Costantinopoli effigiata e descritta*, Turin, 1840. Venice, Biblioteca Nazionale Marciana.

groom. Once alone (or nearly so), the groom donned a sable fur, a gift from the sultana, and escorted by the head of the black eunuchs, was announced to his wife with these words: 'Princess, the pasha, your servant is here', whereupon the eunuch withdrew. The sultana, hidden behind a curtain, waited until her husband said the required prayer, the *namaz*. Then the groom approached, kissed the bride's robe, and awaited her invitation to be seated next to her.

Being married to a sultana was an exacting task for a man. These were the only women in the Empire who were given formal recognition of their superiority over their husbands. When, at the beginning of the eighteenth century, Lady Mary Wortley Montagu visited Turkey, she described the women there as the only free people and saw them as a 'counter-society'. She was probably thinking of the royal princesses, since theirs was the society she frequented as wife of the British ambassador. The symbol of the sultanas' power was the *hançer*, a small sharp dagger studded with precious stones, which they wore at all times attached to their belts. The title they bore was that of *haním sultan*, lady sultan, and even their husbands were required to use it when addressing them.

The princesses could demand total monogamy from their husbands and, when they did so, former concubines of the man were repudiated before the marriage. Nor was the husband allowed to take new slave girls without the prior consent of the lady sultana. Sexual intimacy between man and wife was determined by the will and desire of the sultana.

These ladies had far more autonomy than the sovereign's women and were totally free to receive visits from other ladies of high rank living in Istanbul, both Turks and Europeans. They could visit the Imperial Harem whenever they chose and enjoyed frequent meetings with the sultan in complete privacy. Their credit was high with ministers and they could intercede both for themselves and their protégés. They used this power for good and evil purposes, according to their nature and interests. The names of several of these princesses have come down through the centuries, engraved on the charitable foundations and on the monuments which they erected for the improvement of the city over which they had ruled. However, demands of state also impinged on the existence of these women, for if they did not marry officials such as the grand vizier or a functionary employed in Constantinople, they were separated from their husbands after a few months. The female heirs born from these unions were married off with great honour and generously maintained according to their rank. Male heirs were given a liberal education but could not succeed to the throne nor hold a position at court. The Osmanli dynasty mistrusted relatives and preferred to allocate situations of trust to slaves and eunuchs reared in the palace, people whose life or death depended solely on their faithfulness to their lord.

facing page
Divans covered in cashmere, Persian carpets and tables of mother-of-pearl created an intimate and mysterious atmosphere in the residence of Sait Halim at Istanbul.

A small precious dagger worn attached to the belt was the Ottoman princesses' symbol of power. They were the only women in the Empire whose superiority over their husbands was formally recognized.
Antonio Baratta, *Costantinopoli effigiata e descritta*, Turin, 1840. Venice, Biblioteca Nazionale Marciana.

THE SULTANA MOTHER

On a stifling day in July 1668, Mehpâre Emetüllah Râbia Gülnûs, mother of Sultan Mehmet IV and of Mustafa II, was returning to Istanbul after a short holiday in Hadrianopolis, the beautiful city in Thrace which the Turks used as an outpost during their conquest of the Balkans. She had been born a Christian on the island of Crete, but had converted and become a fevent Muslim.

The French traveller Jean-Baptiste Tavernier, a guest that day in the Ottoman capital, described the solemn entry. At the head of the cortège came small bands of Janissaries, marching as was their custom, without any visible order, plus two hundred knights, rather shabbily dressed, and some of the officials from the royal stables. These were followed by forty knights dressed in pink silk, embellished by elegant velvet quivers of the same colour embroidered with golden lilies. On their heads they wore helmets from which dangled many thin, hairlike chains, which, according to the chronicler, were used to deflect blows in battle. They advanced in a set order: the *ağa* of the Janissaries; six couriers; twelve men in ridiculous garments carrying silver batons on their shoulders; one hundred porters (*kapici*); one hundred guards (*çavuş*) all richly costumed; six hundred gardeners (*bostanci*) with conical hats; two hundred *kadi*, Islamic judges wearing white turbans; two hundred clerics; and many other officials. In front of the carriages, in magnificent robes, there were many black eunuchs mounted on fine horses. At the sides of the carriages were other mounted guards. Râbia Gülnûs, together with another lady, was seated in a carriage drawn by six white horses. On the foot-boards of each carriage were two fierce-looking black eunuchs. Little shutters allowed the princesses to look out without being seen, but nonetheless the officials at the head of the procession motioned the crowd to turn their heads and avert their eyes. The *valide*'s carriage was followed by six coaches carrying her court and her staff. Next to pass were several litters and four carts filled with Bithynian snow to make the ice for the sorbets and drinks which the sultanas consumed in great quantities. The cortège was made up of five thousand people and took three hours to cross the city.

facing page
The courtyard of the *valide* sultan's apartment. She was the absolute sovereign of the harem and ran the establishment with the help of her superintendents and the head of the black eunuchs. The sultana mother organized the social life of the harem, authorizing celebrations and ceremonies, she dictated the lifestyle and administered the considerable income of the harem.
Istanbul, Topkapí.

Besides running the harem, the sultana mother could also take part in politics if she possessed the necessary talent and interest. Many sultanas received foreign ambassadors, supplied references and testimonials and financed public works.
Foggie diverse del vestire de' Turchi,
XV century. Venice, Biblioteca Nazionale Marciana.

Although polygamy was accepted in the Ottoman world, the place of the mother was unique and highly honoured in every family, regardless of social standing. The sultana who had borne the sovereign of sovereigns enjoyed the highest position in the Empire, as well as very special prerogatives. As sultana mother she had power within and outside the seraglio, had great influence on her son and quite often might guide his political decisions and be in contact with foreign states. She was addressed with many titles of respect such as *ippetlu*, 'she who has dignity', and *devetlu*, 'she who has power', but her most common title from the sixteenth century was simply *valide*, 'mother'.

The harem was her private domain. As we have seen, she managed this complex institution with the aid of her superintendents and the chief of the black eunuchs, who was in charge of external relations. The *valide* organized the social life of the harem, arranging receptions, treats, ceremonies, and dictating its

Detail from an Iznick ceramic panel in the apartment of the sultana mother.
Istanbul, Topkapí.

lifestyle. She settled the frequent arguments and administered the considerable revenue from the income that was attributed to the harem. Her own private inheritance, deriving from her imperial dowry, was considerable and she received taxes as well as income from property assigned to her by the sultan whenever a new province was annexed.

The construction of great public works in many of the cities of the Empire was due to the judicious employment of the *valide*'s wealth. The list is a long one, and for Istanbul alone would include the magnificent public baths near Hagia Sophia constructed by Hürrem, or Roxelana, and those of the sultana Cecilia Baffo-Venier at Çemberlitas near Constantine's column, which are still in use. Legend has it that the emperor had the nails of the cross of Christ, together with an effigy of Athena, built into this monument as a kind of symbolic union of the pagan past with the Christian present. The *valide* would also accompany the sultan in the Friday prayers and other religious observances.

The importance of her office was underlined by the majestic ceremony which took place at her installation. The death of a sultan disrupted the composition of the court. In the Empire, high office was given to those who held the personal trust of the sovereign and consequently, at his death, his ministers and grand vizier left the court. As we know, the harem too was affected. The ascent to the throne of the new sulatn was celebrated by the Janissaries, whose duty it was to accompany the heir to the Eyüp Mosque. Here the new lord buckled on the sword, the symbol of his political and religious power, and paid homage to the sacred tomb of Ayyub Ensari, the standard-bearer of the Prophet Mohammed

who died at the foot of the walls of Constantinople. The sultan was accompanied by a huge crowd which silently offered a prayer through the elaborate
screen that hides the sarcophagus of the saint. He then returned to the palace
where the festivities began.

A few days after this ceremony, the installation of the mother of the new sultan
took place. The ceremony, in which a great procession accompanied her to the
imperial residence, was known as the *valide alay.* The Janissaries and the official
who carried the sceptre and the symbols of the Divan preceded the *valide,* who
rode in her carriage followed by her own court. Coins were scattered to the
crowds as they proceeded. Her son awaited her on horseback at the imperial
threshold and greeted her with the ceremonial act of respect which consisted of
kissing the hand three times, then carrying it to the forehead. He then escorted
his mother to the harem. Two days later, via the chief of the black eunuchs, the

sultana would send a sword and a fur to the
grand vizier. The gifts were received and reciprocated with a special ceremony which took
place by the Gate of Salutations.

After all these ceremonies, a new life began.
The queen mother was allowed to change
both the furnishings in her new quarters and
the procedures of her predecessor. She could,
if she was so inclined, take an active role in
politics. It must be remembered that many of
the sultanas were European, and, conscious
of their Christian origins, desired to maintain
good relations with their homelands. In such
instances, they acted as go-betweens for
their country of origin and the lands of the
Crescent, received ambassadors, provided
credentials and recommendations and were
in correspondence with European sovereigns.
The life and fortunes of the *valide* were

Detail of wood and mother-of-pearl
intarsia of a wall cupboard in the
harem.
Istanbul, Topkapí.

ephemeral and dependent upon the fortunes of her son. His early death or
deposition annulled her authority at one stroke. In such circumstances all the
pomp of the installation was reversed, and with no ceremony the *valide* made
the short trip to the old seraglio. Her only comfort in this event might have been
the heart-rending verses of Adni, the pen-name of a powerful sultan:

> *Do not believe in the joys promised by*
>
> *the rotating Celestial Orb in its elusive path,*
>
> *and even if it puts pleasures before your eyes*
>
> *these will be deceptive, for it prepares pain.*

The gates of the Palace of Tears would close forever, like a long wave which
swallows up a ship laden with goods, and after so much prestige, there was only
oblivion as the *valide* awaited death.

A caravanserai built by the *valide* sultan to house goods and travellers. Codice Cicogna, *Memorie turchesche, XVII century*. Venice, Biblioteca del Museo Correr.

A Turkish lady. *Costumi orientali*, XVII century. Bologna, Biblioteca Comunale dell'Archiginnasio.

THE BLACK EUNUCHS, SLAVES OF THE SUBLIME PORTE

Sauntering through the streets of Constantinople with long leisurely strides, the eunuchs would accompany the carriages of the women in their charge. They were round and flaccid, their faces beardless and wrinkled like that of a new born baby; they were tall with long legs but had disproportionately short trunks. They moved alone or in a group, sometimes on foot, sometimes on horseback, glowering fiercely about them to intimidate passersby and discourage any lack of respect toward their charges. The eunuchs were the best source of information for the foreign traveller, since they had an intimate knowledge of the imperial palace and, in exchange for generous gifts, would impart with alacrity the presumed or real secrets in their possession. They have been described with curiosity, as the 'monsters without sex', and pitied for their terrible fate.

Up to the end of the nineteenth century the streets of Istanbul were crowded with eunuchs, as indeed was the whole history of the Ottoman Empire. The origin of the practice of castration is lost in the sands of time. Ancient historians mention castrated slaves throughout the Orient, from Mesopotamia to China. The Persians castrated their Ionian prisoners and offered them, together with virgin girls, as gifts to their sovereigns. Far from eschewing this pagan practice, Christians adopted it until the baroque period, and the high voices of the *castrati* were much in demand for the choir of the Sistine Chapel in Rome. The custom survived until the nineteenth century – as long as the *castrati* were in demand by Italian opera.

Because of the segregation of the sexes in the Arab world, eunuchs were employed, especially in Asia Minor and in the mosques of Mecca and Medina. In the Greek and Byzantine world they were used above all for religious purposes. It was easy for the Ottoman Turks to inherit this Byzantine custom and to adopt it for the care of their women, and, during the time of the Ottoman Empire, every well-to-do family kept at least one pair of eunuchs in its service. Originally the Turks kept only white eunuchs and started using black eunuchs from the sixteenth century, both because of their perceived ugliness and because of their ability to tolerate the operation.

Islam forbids castration, so pious Muslims employed various expedients to assuage their consciences while still enjoying the results. In China eunuchs were always local, whereas in Turkey they were always foreigners; from such Christian lands as Georgia and Armenia, or from Africa, particularly Egypt, the Sudan and Abyssinia.

Traffic in these slaves was lucrative. Merchants usually

facing page
The gate to the black eunuchs' courtyard and detail of a ceramic panel. Ceramic art reached its perfection with the refined techniques of Persia. Ceramic murals created a colourful plane full of movement which allowed architects to broaden the interior space.
Istanbul, Topkapí.

Fat and flabby, with smooth faces and a fierce expression, the eunuchs were continually seen on the streets of Constantinople, either on foot or horseback, following the carriages of the ladies in their care.
Costumi orientali, XVII century. Bologna, Biblioteca Comunale dell'Archiginnasio.

dealt directly with African chiefs, who considered the young men mere merchandise and offered them in vast numbers. Only occasionally were youths sold by their own families out of poverty or greed. From Khartoum to Dongola on the banks of the Nile, from Ethiopia across the Red Sea, these slaves were stowed like sardines in transport ships or ferried by camel caravan, eventually reaching market places in cities in lands bordering the Mediterranean, such as Mecca, Medina, Beirut, Smyrna or Constantinople.

During the journey they were castrated at resting stations, the surgery being performed by Jews or Christians, never by Muslims. The operation was performed without any health precautions, and the only remedy for haemorrhaging was hot desert sand. Mortality was high, but worth the risk on account of the price these slaves fetched. Tavernier, writing at the end of the seventeenth century, noted that a black eunuch was worth up to six hundred *scudi* on the market, and that in Cairo, in Persia or at Constantinople this valuable merchandise often never reached the slave markets but was sold directly to wealthy potentates or to the seraglio itself.

The chief of the black eunuchs in the imperial harem was a person with great influence. He was the right arm and confidential messenger of the sultana mother, and was permitted to approach the sultan without intermediaries, a privilege he shared with few others.
Paul Rycaut, *Istoria dello Stato presente dell'Imperio Ottomano*, Venice, 1672. Venice, Biblioteca Nazionale Marciana.

The techniques used for castration varied and were surrounded by mystery. The penis and testicles were completely removed, the wounds cauterized with boiling oil and for the rest of their lives the *castrati* had to make use of a pipe to urinate. This was kept concealed in their turban, according to Paul Rycaut. Those who had their testicles cut off were known as *spadoni*, while those whose testicles were crushed were known as *thlibae*.

The physical and emotional effects of castration varied according to the age at which it was performed. When carried out before puberty, with the necessary precautions, the risks diminished. After adolescence, the danger of death increased, and the memory of the castration, together with an awareness of an irreparable loss, remained. Eunuchs often retained deep feelings of vengeance, linked to the memory of the violence they had suffered, hatred for both their family and the whole human race, and feelings of inferiority.

By character, eunuchs were, on the whole, petulant, vindictive, cruel and arrogant, while on the other hand they were simple, ingenuous and childlike. Their faces rarely expressed joy, but nearly always anger or boredom. The physical effects of emasculation were evident; they had a woman's voice and are so 'fat, round, flabby, glistening', to use the words of De Amicis in his *Costantinopoli*, 'that they look like blown-up beasts'. Castration also caused insomnia, loss of sight and memory.

The eunuchs drank little alcohol, preferring to indulge in sweets. They became very attached to children and animals, but mostly they were greedy for money which they laboriously sought to accumulate, possibly in order to feel more powerful and to compensate for the great void which surrounded their existence.

They loved music and dance, and the black eunuchs remained attached to the rhythms and spirit of their African homeland. They dressed with great elegance, in clean and expensive clothes and perfumed themselves like vain women. When they entered the seraglio each took a new name in relation to the women they guarded: Hyacinth, Rose, Narcissus or Carnation, in order to evoke by their names the odour of flowers, virginity and purity.

Despite the precautions taken by jealous Turks, the use of eunuchs to guard their women did not automatically eliminate every risk of sexual activity. Castration did not remove all sexual desire, and a eunuch who had not been fully castrated could take pleasure in a woman and be free from any danger of pro-creation, a considerable advantage in a clandestine affair with a woman entrusted to his care. Occasionally children castrated at a very tender age redeveloped what they had lost, so in order to avoid any unpleasant surprises, the doctors of the imperial seraglio carried out a rigorous inspection not only at the time of admission, but repeated it every couple of years. Since the eunuchs had frequent contact with the outside world, they were able to pro-cure both aphrodisiacs and sexual aids which helped to compensate for what they lacked.

The complete and continuous absence of sexual opportunities in the rigidly controlled seraglio resulted in 'intimacies condemned by Nature'. Homosexual love flourished in the harems, especially among the young, who were neither positively discouraged nor forced to moderate their ardour, despite some danger of punish-ment and the vigilance of the old eunuchs. The vice of Sodom had followers in the Ottoman Empire even among certain sultans, who made no secret of their inclinations. With typical Venetian crude-ness, Secretary Marcantonio Donini described the fat and glutto-nous Sultan Selim II, who 'had women and boys whom he desired brought to him either with their consent or by force'. In these sur-roundings relationships often developed between women and eunuchs. In some instances they were allowed to marry and live outside the harem, but this was almost always only in the case of eunuchs who had reached a very high rank.

The white and black eunuchs of the Topkapí had different jobs, lived in separate quarters and were allowed to come together only on special occasions. The white eunuchs were in the service of the sultan and were educated alongside the *acemi oğlan*, the youths in the external service of the administration. They lived in the Third Court in buildings facing the sides of the Gate of Felicity and their supreme head was the *kapí ağasí*, the grand master. It was he who introduced ambassadors at an audience, who compiled writings and memoirs, and accom-panied his lord everywhere. The close contact with the sultan which the grand masters enjoyed put them in a position of great authority, power and prestige.

EUNUCHS, THE CUSTODIANS OF HAPPINESS

There is no need to have them pointed out; they are immediately recognizable. They wear a fez, a long dark overcoat, European-style trousers and carry a whip of hippopotamus hide, the symbol of their office. They walk with great long strides, feebly, like great big babies. They accompany women on foot or on horseback, preceding or following their carriages, sometimes singly, sometimes in pairs, and keep a wary eye out for any glance or other act of disrespect from passersby, at which point they assume a savage expression which instils fear and repugnance. Otherwise their faces reveal nothing at all, or express at most an infinite boredom with everything. I cannot remember once seeing a eunuch laugh.

De Amicis, *Costantinopoli*, 1877

A lady on horseback, accompanied by her black slave.
George De La Chappelle, *Recuel de divers portraits*, Paris, 1648. Venice, Biblioteca Nazionale Marciana.

The chief of the black eunuchs at the Topkapí dressed in a precious caftan lined with fur. His title was 'Pasha with Three Tails', and he received a rich endowment. He was permitted to have for his exclusive use both eunuchs and women slaves.
Raccolta di 120 stampe, Venetiis, 1783.
Venice, Biblioteca Nazionale Marciana.

There was a strict hierarchy governing the standing of the white eunuchs, and the older and more experienced ones attended upon the sultan. Other white eunuchs were entrusted with the goods that arrived at court from every province of the Empire: ambergris from Yemen; musk and theriacas from Cairo; silk from Bursa and muslin and other cloth from India; as well as agates, turquoise, diamonds and crystals and other goods of great value. The duties of the white eunuchs ended at the doors of the women's quarter and did not extend throughout the palace.

The harem was served exclusively by black eunuchs from Africa chosen for their ugliness and deformities so as to discourage any interest whatsoever on the part of the women. They were often sent as gifts from the governors of Cairo and, after careful selection, the youths who had been completely castrated were gathered in the quarters of the harem reserved for them. Here they were strictly disciplined, fiercely beaten by their superiors and harshly taught how to perform their duties. Their job was to control the people who came in and out of the harem, to accompany the women on their rare excursions outside the palace, and to act as go-betweens with the outside world, conveying messages and orders to the *selamlík* or to court dignitaries.

The black eunuchs were organized in a complex hierarchy. At the head was the superintendent of the girls, or *kízlar ağasí*, the right arm of the queen mother and the minister in charge of the external dealings of the sultana. He had many duties, was part of the *valide*'s council, and together with her filled vacancies in the harem. He oversaw the education of the princes and the princesses and was the confidential messenger of the queen mother. He could approach the sultan without intermediaries, a privilege enjoyed by few, had the lucrative position of inspector, or *vakíf*, of the charitable foundations and was the head of the halberdiers, the *baltací*. He was responsible for providing concubines for the harem, pronounced death sentences and oversaw the execution of women who had committed crimes.

This head of the black eunuchs carried the title of 'Pasha with Three Tails' and wore a precious uniform adorned with many furs. He received rich endowments, had three hundred horses for his exclusive use and could keep both eunuchs and women as slaves. His unique position allowed him to accumulate huge wealth by more or less legitimate means. It was rare for such a highly ranked person to give up his job voluntarily, but when this happened the sultan provided a considerable pension for the slave and sent him to Egypt to finish his life in splendour. Even though he held such high office the *kízlar ağasí* was almost always without any education or fine taste.

Following the *ağa* in the hierarchy came the treasurer, or *hazinedar ağa*, who took care of the finances of the harem and the halberdiers. He also had the title of 'Pasha with Three Tails' and succeeded the *kízlar ağasí* in case of the latter's death or demotion. Then came the *bas, musahib* the chamberlain who was the contact between the sultan and the *kízlar ağasí*. The chamberlain had eight to ten eunuchs under him who were charged with taking the orders and messages

from the sultan to his ladies. The *baş kapí oğlan*, or first officer, also had an important function controlling the various apartments.

The power of the eunuchs was kept under control as long as the structure of the Ottoman Empire remained firm. At the end of the sixteenth century, however, the sultans no longer governed the state directly from the imperial palace. They no longer took part in military expeditions, contributed little to the development of art and culture and ceased to govern properly, giving themselves over to the pleasures of the harem and to an unfruitful and dissolute life. Gone was the time when heaven cast no shadow on this state upon which it had bestowed so many favours, and the Sublime Porte began to experience corruption and poor government, leading to an institutional and economic crisis. Power passed from the sultan to a palace cabal, and throughout the seventeenth century the eunuchs and the *valide* were in control politically.

In the nineteenth century, inefficient and corrupt practices began to be discarded and the lands of the Crescent renewed itself, thanks to progressive Western ideas. The power of the eunuchs declined with the 'happy reforms' of the waning Empire. They viewed with fear the approaching new regime which instituted incomprehensible changes. A telling episode occurred at the end of the nineteenth century. A eunuch was accompanying two women from the Imperial Harem on a shopping expedition when their carriage met a French officer riding across the Galata bridge. The two women, excited by the greater sense of freedom circulating in Constantinople, flirtatiously blew kisses at him. The officer reciprocated and the eunuch, who saw what had happened, struck the Frenchman with his whip. The officer immediately unsheathed his sword and without hesitation killed the eunuch in the presence of the stunned crowd. In earlier times, this action would have had grave consequences, but, on this occasion, the Ottoman government accepted the version of the French commanding officer, who justified the behaviour of his officer by saying that he had been obliged to defend himself against the offensive provocation of a black man.

Once they were no longer politically in control, the duties of these servants were limited to giving or withholding permission to ladies wishing to visit the harem and to escorting their mistresses who, encouraged by the winds of change, increasingly wanted to go shopping in the main bazaar of the city. When harems were abolished by law, the eunuchs no longer had a role and suddenly found themselves without privilege or power, victims of the new regime.

facing page
Servants and functionaries of the Sublime Porte. *Above*, the head cook and other attendants of the imperial kitchens. *Below*, a 'Pasha with Three Tails' and his assistants.
Giulio Ferrario, *Il Costume antico e moderno*, Milan, 1828. Venice, Biblioteca Nazionale Marciana.

Flowers and fruit for the ladies of the harem being carried by an imperial page.
Costumi orientali, XVII century. Bologna, Biblioteca Comunale dell'Archiginnasio.

following pages
European extravaganza and Islamic furniture mingled together in the home of Sait Halim and revealed the same ambivalence towards progress and tradition that was apparent in Ottoman politics in the eighteenth century.

THE HOUSE OF FELICITY

Smoking was a necessity for the Turks, who spared no expense in procuring top-quality tobacco. Théophile Gautier wrote that Constantinople was perpetually enveloped in a cloud of smoke, like this fascinating concubine without her veil.
Jean Lecomte du Nouy, *The White Slave*, 1888. Nantes, Musée des Beaux-Arts.

FOOD, SWEETS AND SORBETS

In the seraglio, food was not a matter of secondary importance; it was a constant source of delight made all the more pleasurable by a complicated ritual for its consumption. The dishes served at the imperial table were infinitely more refined and varied than those of ordinary people. In the lands of the Crescent, most people existed on fairly sober and ordinary food, such as marrow, melons and fresh fruit in the summer, rice and soups in the winter.

The Ottoman capital was favoured by a policy of protectionism towards the supply of provisions, and was where consumer goods arriving from every province of the Empire were sorted out. The top-quality produce went to the palace. Some of the villages on the outskirts of Constantinople, which depended directly on the imperial estates, as well as a vast network of merchants, supplied goods on a daily basis to the steward in charge of the sultan's kitchens. To this were added many luxury foods imported from abroad.

At the Topkapí about one hundred lambs and two hundred sheep from the Balkans, the Anatolian plateau and the Taurus Mountains of Cilicia were consumed every day, and about two hundred and thirty hens, chickens and geese from Thrace and Izmir. Beef was not much in demand except for dried and salted cuts from calving cows, which were preserved throughout the year in huge vats. Oil came from Greece, but for the women of the harem only the finest, light and odourless oil from Candia was used.

Honey was consumed in vast quantities at the Sublime Porte and used in the preparation of many dishes, not only compotes and sorbets. This delicacy, a substitute for sugar, was part of an

A pitcher of nomadic design, richly set
with precious stones.
Istanbul, Topkapí.

annual tribute paid to the sultan by his vassals in Walachia, Transylvania and Moldavia. Butter was rarely used fresh; it was prepared in large ox hearts and then shipped from the Black Sea. Biscuits and sugared almonds came from Venice, but the ladies of the court particularly appreciated the delicate cheeses of Piacenza and Lombardy, which the Venetian ambassador imported in considerable quantities. Lemons, oranges and limes came from Chios; dates from Asia; salt from Egypt; cherries from the Black Sea; peaches and apricots from Sinop; pears and figs from the Bosporus; vegetables, spices and sugar crystals from Alexandria; and from the neighbourhood of Istanbul came yoghurt. Fish was not often eaten but when required could be obtained in abundance: sole, mackerel, sea bass, oysters and crab. The Island of the Princes and the Belgrade Forest near the capital provided game, but this was not particularly relished by the Turks.

A vast quantity of food ended up in the imperial kitchens, where cooks and kitchen boys worked relentlessly at top speed to supply their master's needs. Black eunuchs carried dishes to the harem for the meals that were consumed in the morning, at midday and in the evening. Despite fairy tales believed in the West, the sultanas did not eat off gold plates, for even the sultan respected the Koranic law, although at court there was tableware in thick gold and set with precious stones. The ladies ate off scrupulously clean tin-plated copper or porcelain dishes. Cutlery was not used, and up to the reign of Mahmut II, at the beginning of the nineteenth century, food was eaten using the hands. The novices were taught this art, which they were required to perform with grace and delicacy. Turkish cuisine, in fact, did not really require eating implements, since the meat, always very tender and well cooked, was served in small pieces and bread could be used to take food from the plate. Wooden or

THE GRAND TURK'S LUNCHEON

As the moment for the Grand Turk's meal draws near, the young men of his private pantry set two cloths in a basket to hold the lord's bread. They fill many silver jars with Turkish drinks such as juleps, sugared water, or water flavoured with mastic and, in the same way, without further settings, they assemble many little porcelain dishes flavoured with mint, violets and other herbs, and fruit compotes prepared in their fashion, and carry these into the room where the king wishes to dine. The Grand Turk settles on the floor, seated on carpets with his legs crossed one over the other, and the servant serves him kneeling before him. And when the lord wishes to drink, one of the three favoured youths hands him a cup made of the bark of coconut encased in gold bands. The Grand Turk always eats alone and no one enters the room while he is eating. And he never eats off gold or silver although he has superb dinner services made of these. In summer it is customary for him to eat three times a day, that is in the morning, at noon and in the evening. In winter he eats twice a day. After his meal he is entertained by clowns for a short while, and then he goes off to sleep.

Menavino, *I Costumi e la vita dei Turchi*, 1551

Pitcher and tray
Istanbul, Topkapí.

preceding pages
The chimneys and cupolas of the great Topkapí kitchens look towards the vast stretches of Constantinople, city of dreams and the pearl of the Orient.

tortoiseshell spoons were used for soups and sorbets. At the end of the meal servants brought bowls for the washing of fingers.

As in all Turkish mansions, no room in the Imperial Harem was used specifically for dining. In nomadic fashion, the dwelling was considered a single area in which all daily activities took place. The servants brought the dishes to the pavilion where the women had gathered. Huge trays called *tabla*, placed on low stools covered with a cloth, served as tables. Napkins were replaced by richly embroidered handkerchiefs. Those sharing the meal sat Turkish-style on sofas, rather wide little low divans, which at night were used for sleeping. Each meal was a social occasion, and often the sultanas invited their friends to join them, and when the great lord spent a whole day in the harem he would attend the banquets with his concubines and favourites. Usually, the sultan had his meals alone and conversed with no one. From time to time he was joined by his doctor and occasionally mutes and clowns entertained him with their pranks.

A long succession of dishes was brought in, one after the other, since the Ottomans enjoyed picking at many rather than gorging on a few dishes. Their nomadic frugality at the table had been replaced by Byzantine refinement; although Turkish cuisine retained the flavour of its nomadic origins in the Anatolian plateau, it acquired as it went along a variety of nuances. To the traditional *kebab* meat dishes, and *pilaf* rice dishes of Central Asia, were added *dolma*, stuffed vegetables particularly enjoyed by the Seljuk Turks, and several cold dishes dressed in olive oil invented by the Ottomans.

Meat was usually roasted, but also boiled or cooked in butter, oil or apple sauces. Dripping and lard were not used, since pork was forbidden to Muslims. Many dishes contained opium, cabbage, marrow, spinach and onion. Together with

Waiters ready to serve two stately inhabitants of Constantinople with their pipes, coffee, sugared almonds, incense and rose water.
Giulio Ferrario, *Il Costume antico e moderno*, Milan, 1828. Venice, Biblioteca Nazionale Marciana.

salads and vegetables came the delicious *börek*, layers of light pastry filled with cheese and then fried. Aubergine and courgettes were stuffed with meat and rice and served hot or cold, either salted or in a sweet and sour sauce. Tender vine leaves were used to wrap tiny *dolma*, olives and pickles called *turşu* were always on the table, and the meal ended with *pilaf* rice, considered by Tavernier the most delicious of all Eastern dishes: he included a recipe for it in his *Relatione*.

Many types of bread were made, and the bakery of the seraglio produced the whitest bread for the sultan, the sultanas and those of very high rank; the quality of bread declined as the recipients moved down the social ladder. The wheat, as a rule, came from Greece, but for the royal palate only the best flour was used, and that was grown on the sovereign's estates in Bursa, in the province of Bithynia. Bread was dusted with opium, cumin and other spices, which gave it a certain piquancy, and there were many types of rolls: thin plain flat bread, dough made with butter and coated with beaten egg, and bland white bread which, though much appreciated in the seraglio, was described by the traveller Luigi Bassano as 'mortar under one's teeth'. Drinks were served not during the meal but after it. Diners drank from a communal crystal goblet into which they dipped large spoons. The rich never drank water, but enjoyed instead delicious nectars and stimulants known as *serbets*, much liked by the Europeans who borrowed both the drink and the name (the word 'sorbet' comes from *serbet*). These drinks were made of sugared water flavoured with lime, apple, pear or prune juice and essences from flowers and herbs: violets, roses, saffron, mint or linden. The ladies also loved to add the precious essences of musk, ambergris and aloe. Some stronger-tasting sorbets were made of barley or millet, and one in particular was made with the liquid distilled from a horseshoe-shaped plant, *nilüfer* or ninfea, a water lily with huge yellow flowers that grows in marshes, streams and garden ponds.

Prior to a visit to the sultanas, the Ottoman sultans put aphrodisiacs in their sorbets, and court officials used secretly to bribe the supervisor of the sorbets to obtain these magic potions. Much appreciated at a Turkish meal were compotes of stewed fruits flavoured with musk or ambergris. In the House of Felicity a great quantity of fruits, flowers and spices were consumed, and the staff in charge of the provisions always ensured that the larders were well stocked. The sorbets, kept in porcelain and crystal jars, were prepared by the pastry chefs, who worked in rooms above the kitchens. Turkish drinks were delicate and varied and more care was taken in their preparation than that of food. Sorbets were drunk cold, and ice to cool them was imported from Mount Olympus near Bursa. The snow

The Turks ate with their hands and did not use cutlery except for a few travellers who had brought back these strange luxury items from Europe. Their cuisine does not require knives and forks, only large spoons for soup or sorbets. The principal dish is rice *pilaf*.
Jean Lecomte du Nouy, *The White Slave*, detail, 1888. Nantes, Musée des Beaux-Arts.

A RECIPE FOR PILAF RICE

A sufficient quantity of mutton, or chicken or pigeons is taken according to the number of persons to be served. These are boiled in a pan or crock until they are partially cooked and then everything, that is, both meat and broth, are emptied into a little basin. The same pan is put over the fire with enough butter which must be well heated, while one cuts the partially cooked meat into small pieces, that is, the chicken into quarters, the pigeons in half. This meat then is put in the butter and fried until it becomes nicely browned.

The rice, which has been selected and well washed, is kept ready, and one puts it in the pan over the meat, as much as is deemed necessary, and over this one pours the broth from the basin, with a spoon, until it rises a finger's breadth over the rice. One covers the pan and sets it over a bright flame and when it has boiled for some time one takes a few grains of rice to see if they are soft and cooked, pouring on it from time to time more of the broth to finish off the cooking.

Their rice is different from ours because it does not burst when it is overcooked, just like their pepper corns, which are used whole. At the right moment one firmly covers the pan with a cloth folded over five or six times and puts a dish on top. Then little by little one melts more butter to pour into it, having made holes in the rice with the handle of the spoon, quickly covering it to allow it to swell and fully absorb all the liquid. Then it is brought to the table. It is served on large platters with the meat carefully arranged on top. At times it is served white, at times coloured yellow with saffron, at times tinged red with pomegranate juice.

Tavernier, *Relatione del Seraglio*, 1682

from the ice fields, wrapped in heavy cloths, was transported by mules and it reached the seraglio only after several days' journey. The eccentric Turkish traveller Evliya Çelebi described how mountaineers from Olympus arriving in the crowded capital city with their turbans covered in snow, were regarded as astonishing creatures. *Pekmez*, made from reduced grape juice, was also very popular, as was *hosaf*, a drink made from raisins steeped in water to which were added mead and rose water.

Desserts and syrups prepared by pastry cooks were creative and delicious and were consumed in great quantities by the women. Semolina tarts dripping with honey and garnished with coconut and pistachios; complicated soups made of figs, apricots, wheat, chick peas and beans, mixed with rose water; delicate cream of almond puddings; or chicken meat puréed in milk; light pastry covered in honey and raisins: all these carried names which evoked hidden and intimate feminine characteristics and attributes.

TURKISH CUISINE

Wanting to learn something of Turkish cuisine, I had myself taken to an *ad hoc* eating place where every kind of oriental dish could be got, from the most exquisite delicacies of the Seraglio to camel meat cooked Arab style and horse meat done the Turcoman way. We were brought about twenty dishes...but I could not describe each in detail because most of what I retained was a vague, rather sinister impression.

There were many little dishes of lamb and mutton, cooked to shreds and boiled for so long that they had lost all flavour. There were fish swimming in oil, rice balls wrapped in vine leaves, marrow in syrup, mixed salads, compotes, preserves, sauces flavoured with every sort of aromatic herb, as numerous as the articles of the penal code for relapsed criminals. Then at the end of the meal a huge plate of sweets was brought, the chef d'oeuvre of some Arab pastry cook, which included a miniature ship, a fanciful lion and a little house made of sugar with tiny latticed windows. All in all I felt that I had emptied into my stomach the entire contents of a physician's portmanteau.

De Amicis, *Costantinopoli*, 1878

Under the attentive gaze of a eunuch, one of the favourites entertains her lord with music.
Antonio Baratta, *Costantinopoli effigiata e descritta*, Turin, 1840. Venice, Biblioteca Nazionale Marciana.

SENSUAL DELIGHTS:

COFFEE, TOBACCO AND OPIUM

Life in the harem flowed without haste in the enjoyment of all sensual delights. The girls were busy making music, enjoying flowers and delicately flavoured drinks and food, but the slow rhythm of the day favoured most the joys of idleness and the pleasure of conversation. In the best Eastern tradition, uncalled-for troubles and cares were frowned upon, as were any bustle and unnecessary comings and goings. In this indolent, contemplative life, stimulating drinks and drugs were eagerly desired.

When Lady Wortley Montagu visited the harem of Hafiza, the favourite of Sultan Ahmet III, she was given a superb reception. The meal, as was the custom, consisted of fifty or so courses presented one after the other and ending with sorbet served in Chinese porcelain dishes. After the meal, coffee was served by charming slave girls in wonderful Japanese coffee cups with golden saucers, in a room perfumed by the inebriating essence of ambergris and aloe, to the soothing sounds of sweet music.

The visit was in March 1718 and coffee was very much in vogue both in Europe and in the East. Two centuries earlier, when the drink had been introduced to Turkey, many had held it suspect because it was thought to affect the mind. The Venetian Gianfrancesco Morosini, on his return from Constantinople in 1585, told his fellow citizens with a certain amount of amazement about the Turkish custom of drinking a boiling black liquid 'which is obtained from a seed called Caveè, which they say has the virtue of keeping a man awake'. This 'healthiest of drinks' was destined to become popular and despite the opposition of certain pious Muslims and the prohibitions of certain sultans, many coffee shops were opened in Istanbul. Thanks to the land of the Crescent, coffee, which was first sold in Europe as a medicinal plant, soon became a highly popular drink, particularly in France and Venice.

A young woman drinking coffee, a rite of the harem that was repeated frequently throughout the day.
Raccolta di 120 stampe, Venetiis, 1783.
Venice, Biblioteca Nazionale Marciana.

In the harem, drinking coffee was a pleasant ritual which was repeated many times during the day. Reclining on wide sofas after a meal or in the relaxing atmosphere of the baths, either during the day or the long night, women sipped this well-known black drink; unlike today, it was never drunk at breakfast. Turkish coffee is prepared from almost pulverized beans mixed with cold water and sugar and then boiled. Its preparation required skill on the part of the slave girls, who had to learn both to make it and serve it correctly.

While coffee came to be generally used, a completely different attitude was taken towards alcoholic beverages, which were officially forbidden to all Muslims: it was particularly inappropriate for women to drink wine and liquor. Wine was vigorously prohibited up to the rule of Süleyman, who had all wine vats burned, but neither

From a youthful age both women and
men smoked these long pipes and
narghile (hookah) at home and on
the street.
Turchia Album di 62 foto, n.d. Venice,
Biblioteca Nazionale Marciana.

facing page
Narghile were made of gold, silver and
chiselled steel. They were as elegant as
ancient vases and enriched by
turquoises, coral and other gems. A
scented tobacco was smoked in these
masterpieces, which brought the
smoker happy hours of oblivion.
Ange Tissier, *An Algerian Woman and her
Slave*, 1860. Paris, Musée National des Arts
d'Afrique et d'Oceanie.

prohibition nor taxes managed to stop its consumption, and many bars and taverns existed in Istanbul. The people as well as grandees enjoyed their forbidden liquor. The unhappy Prince Cem, a prisoner at the Papal Court, drowned his miserable fettered life in wine, while Baqi, a prince among poets, sang verses in praise of the goblet. As attitudes relaxed, wine was allowed into the House of Felicity and from the time of Selim II, who passed into history as Sarhos, 'The Sot', many other sultans gave in to the temptation of alcohol. The wines that came to Istanbul were mainly produced in the Ottoman provinces of Thrace, Smyrna and on the isle of Tenedos, but Italian, French, Spanish and Hungarian wines were also imported. Those who drank appreciated *raki,* or *arak,* also known as 'lion's milk', a drink flavoured with aniseed. Its manufacture was left to Armenian infidels, who exported it from Çorlu in Thrace. By this means Muslims managed to overcome the law forbidding the manufacture of alcohol, and *raki,* a refreshing drink when diluted and only inebriating if drunk neat, could be sold in great quantities.

The taste for tobacco spread throughout the East during the reign of Mehmet III at the end of the sixteenth century. At home and abroad both men and women smoked long pipes (*çubuk*) and hookahs. Sweets, sorbets, coffee and tobacco were necessary accompaniments during the long hours of conversation. Pietro della Valle noted that the Turks played a thousand little games with smoke, which seemed to amuse them, while the traveller found it 'a disgusting habit'. The women of the seraglio consumed a lot of tobacco, mixing it with the wood of aloe and, to make it sweeter, a resinous gum known as mastic, produced from the mastic trees of Chios. This yellow resin had an aromatic taste as well as a pleasant smell and was said to be good for the gums, to cure stomach pains and toothache and to check haemorrhaging. Mastic was also chewed alone and was sometimes used to perfume cups before coffee was poured into them.

To combat the boredom of life at the palace the women used several drugs including *theriacus*, known as Galen's ecstasy, but above all they favoured opium, which 'brings happiness and removes all worry'. Opium, produced in great quantities in Asia Minor, was taken as an infusion, chewed or smoked in a pipe. An elaborate version, in which musk, ambergris and other essences were added, was often preferred. In the House of Felicity the favourite method of opium consumption was in the form of tablets to which powdered pearls, lapis lazuli, rubies and emeralds were added. Most women chose to chew rather than smoke because the effect was longer-lasting. In the long night watches, the 'elixir of the night' granted the women of the harem an illusion of freedom from the golden cage that was the Imperial Palace.

A precious pitcher.
Istanbul, Topkapí.

A female slave who was favoured by the sultan at the peak of her youthful beauty was supposed to remain enticing for many years. The art of beautification was widely practised in the seraglio and, in order to help nature and appear attractive, women used all sorts of remedies and were willing to spend considerable sums on creams, tinctures, jewels, clothing, perfumes and footware. Beautiful costumes were worn, and the court of the Lords of the Bosporus was resplendent with garments to satisfy the Asiatic taste for luxurious clothing and fulfill the requirements for pomp and splendour at official ceremonies. Each wardrobe was renewed once a season and the princesses never wore the same dress twice.

Early sultans paid great attention to regulations governing dress and the colour of clothes and turbans, in order to maintain clear class distinctions. After the conquest of Constantinople, however, the consumption of luxury goods grew, thanks to the influence of Byzantine elegance. According to Western travellers, apart from their headgear, men and women dressed in more or less the same manner, an impression created by the fact that both sexes wore wide trousers and long shirts. When women left the house they would cover themselves with a veil and tunic, a Koranic injunction to avoid causing temptation; in fact, this merely encouraged fantasies and led to even greater dangers. So dressed, the entire female population moved about in complete freedom and anonymity. If, as De Amicis wrote, their veils were to fall off by magic, our conviction of their uniformity would also vanish, and we would discover 'Turkish women dressed as Asian queens, others like French women, some as grand merchant ladies, food peddlers, horsewomen, Greeks or gypsies'.

The uniform appearance of the *ferace* was only superficial. It was long and shapeless and reached down to the ankles, but the uniforms for outings had distinct variations. Those of the working class were made of black cloth, while high-class women wore pink, lilac and other strong colours, enriched by embroideries. In summer *feraces* were made of silk, in winter of thicker cloth. This constant masquerade which transformed Istanbul into a giant stage was made even more theatrical by the wearing of the *yaşmak*, or veil.

The fine muslin *yaşmak* was made in two parts: the first covered the mouth and the nose, the second was wrapped around the head. Only the eyes were uncovered, for unlike their Arab contemporaries, Ottoman women did not wear a mask over their eyes. The most severe regulations were in force for the imperial ladies; in the classic era of the Empire, they had to be completely veiled when they went out, but in time this custom too was modified. The much-reviled garb could not hide bewitching glances nor natural grace, and women managed to be flirtatious even under the wary eye of the eunuchs, pretending to smooth their dress or casually letting a handkerchief drop. They had learned to communicate despite their clothing and allowed the colours to speak for them: blue for a meeting, black for separation.

The most typical part of a Turkish woman's attire was the wide trousers which narrowed down to the ankle. These *şalvar* were made of fine brocade from Bursa, of damask or silk in vivid shades. Trousers were embroidered with silver flowers and worn over long underwear called *dizlik*. The long shirt, with wide pointed sleeves, fell limply over the pants. It was made of wool, cotton, or a more costly material such as silk, and fastened at the neck by a showy jewel. White was the preferred colour, but red, yellow and turquoise were also worn. On their feet women wore *babusch*, soft kid slippers of Moroccan leather, and at home soft slippers decorated with pearls and precious stones and with a slight curve at the toes.

Another important garment was the *entari*, a sort of waistcoat fitting at the waist, which could be worn buttoned or open as fashion dictated. Usually it was embellished by pearl or diamond buttons. Then there was the caftan, a garment with wide sleeves that reached the ankle, sometimes made of the same material as the trousers. Turkish women did not wear gloves, but wide belts, made of wool, silk or linen, which they used to hold handkerchiefs and money, were an important accessory. The type of belt indicated the woman's status; sultanas and other ladies of high rank wore belts covered in diamonds and pearls, while poorer ladies embellished theirs with embroidery. All women of standing had a diamond buckle for their belt.

In winter the ladies of the seraglio wore heavy brocade capes, trimmed and lined with sable and mink. Not only the ladies wore furs: eunuchs, courtiers and the sultans themselves wore lined caftans and spared no expense to line their caftans with the best furs that came to Istanbul from Russia via the port of Tanus. They also wore the *kalpak*, a fur hat, occasionally made of heavy velvet bordered with pearls. For the summer these were of lighter, brightly coloured material.

The Asian hairstyle was considered the most beautiful in the world. Black hair was preferred and those women who were not so endowed used henna to dye it red. As the writer Luigi Bassano maliciously reported: those who 'don't have it by

Precious sixteenth-century Turkish fabrics.
Venice, Private Collection.

nature get it by skill'. Lady Mary Wortley Montagu wrote that she had counted one hundred and ten braids on the head of one lady, 'all of them real'. It is to her that we owe the following description: 'The headdress is composed of a cap…fixed on one side of the head, hanging a little way down with a golden tassle and bound on, either with a circle of diamonds (as I have seen several) or a rich embroidered handkerchief. On the other side of the head the hair is laid flat; and here the ladies are at liberty to shew their fancies; some putting flowers, others a plume of heron's feathers, and in short, what they please; but the most general fashion is a large *bouquet* of jewels made like real flowers; that is, the buds, of pearl; the roses, of different coloured rubies; the jessamines, of diamonds; the jonquils, of topazes etc. so well set and enamelled, 'tis hard to imagine any thing of that kind so beautiful. The hair hangs at its full length behind, divided into tresses braided with pearl or ribbon, which is always in great quantity'.

Turkish women had a real passion for ornaments: rings, brooches, bracelets and necklaces. The imperial goldsmiths created magnificent jewellery for the court ladies and when Ottoman pieces were deemed unsatisfactory, foreign merchants made up the deficiency. The sultanas owned an amazing quantity of jewels. Ottomans even had their arms, armour and domestic objects so thickly encrusted with jewels that their original shape was obscured. What mattered most was how much the piece had cost: stones were often uncut, but enormous and applied in the 'barbaric' fashion, for chromatic effect rather than delicate detail. Such everyday objects as mirrors, cups and pitchers were decorated with jewels. In the elegant seraglio, luxuries of every kind were scattered around: finely carved ornaments, mirrors encrusted with pearls, nightcaps sewn with diamonds, sables thrown casually across a sofa, Isfahan carpets and brocade cushions. Clearly it was here that life – in the sense of pleasure and intimacy – was fully enjoyed.

facing page
Various fashions: *above*, ladies dressed in summer, spring and winter attire in the company of a woman from a lower class, who was not allowed to wear fur-lined garments. *Below*, veiled Muslim ladies and European ladies. Giulio Ferrario, *Il Costume antico e moderno*, Milan, 1828. Venice, Biblioteca Nazionale Marciana.

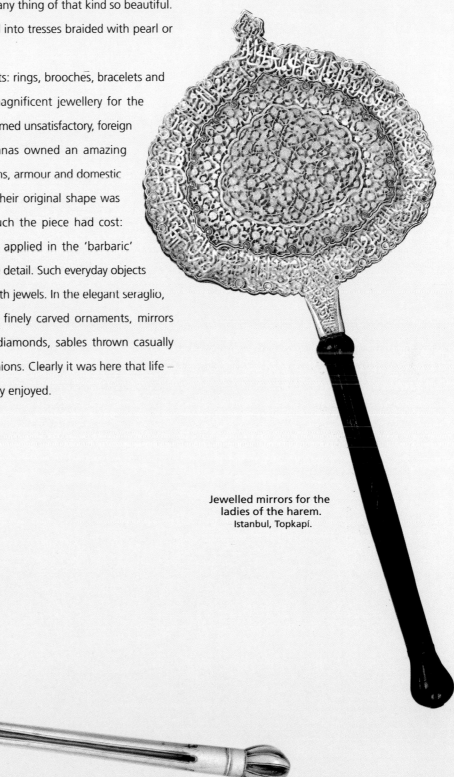

Jewelled mirrors for the ladies of the harem. Istanbul, Topkapí.

THE WOMEN'S COFFEE HOUSE

Less wealthy Turks frequented the public baths while the rich enjoyed this pastime in their own homes.
Jean-Auguste Ingres, *The Turkish Bath*, 1812. Paris, Musée du Louvre.

Woman washing in the *hamam*. The Greco-Roman tradition of the baths remained intact in the East because ablutions and the cleansing of the body are an obligation imposed by the Koran.
Costumi orientali, XVII century. Bologna, Biblioteca Comunale dell'Archiginnasio.

Turkish women spent endless time in the baths – washing, being massaged and having superfluous hair removed. Lower-class women went to public baths while the rich ladies and the sultan's women enjoyed this convenience at home. In the imperial seraglio there were several baths equipped with every comfort in keeping with the luxury of the place. The structure of Turkish hamams derived from Byzantium. But while they were smaller than Roman baths, the arrangement was more flexible and the furnishings more luxurious and comfortable. The use of temperate saunas allowed bathers to stay up to two hours or so, and women ordered fruit and drinks which they consumed as they talked.

In these lovely stone buildings, lighted by small apertures in the cupola, women gave themselves over to beautifying their bodies. They discarded their clothes in a large dressing room, the *camekân*, corresponding to the Roman *apoditerium*, and then rested in the *tepidarium* to get accustomed to the warmer temperature. They then proceeded to the *sïcaklïk* or *calidarium*, a vast hall decorated in Marmara marble or with Iznik tiles, with fountains placed along the walls. In the centre was a heated platform for massage. There was constant cold and hot running water, since Turks did not use tubs, whose standing water might harbour *jinn*, the well-known evil imps of the Muslim world.

Seated on low marble benches set along the walls, the women were soaped and washed by slaves. The *tellâk*, servants of the baths, were skilled at combing and braiding hair, as well as rubbing the skin with a rough glove. To remove all grease from the hair, they used a perfumed soap and *kil*, a type of clay that was kneaded with rose petals. The body was also rubbed with cloves and ginger, a cosmetic the odalisques were convinced had no equal for increasing their powers of seduction. Naked, relaxed and idle in the luxurious surroundings, the Turkish princesses were not restrained by the puritanism of the Christian world. They could give themselves up to full enjoyment of their bodies, without shame or feeling the need to hide either their charms or their blemishes, and behaved with a spontaneity unknown to their European counterparts.

behaved with a spontaneity unknown to their European counterparts.

Lady Wortley Montagu, who could not miss out on such an exciting experience, described her visit to a *hamam* in Hadrianopolis with a touch of irony. 'I believe, upon the whole, there were two hundred women, and yet none of those disdainful smiles and satirical whispers, that never fail in our assemblies, when any body appears that is not dressed exactly in the fashion... The first sofas were covered in cushions and rich carpets, on which sat the ladies; and on the second, their slaves behind them, but without any distinction of rank by their dress, all being in the state of nature, that is, in plain English stark naked, without any beauty or defect concealed...There were many amongst them as exactly proportioned as ever any goddess was drawn by the pencil of a Guido or Titian – and most of their skins shiningly white, only adorned by their beautiful hair divided into many tresses, hanging on their shoulders, braided either with pearl or ribbon, perfectly representing the figures of the Graces.' The English guest, in her riding habit, was persuaded to 'open [her] shirt' and, upon revealing her tight corset, was pitied by the Turkish women who believed it was a chastity belt which her husband obliged her to wear and into which she was locked.

The women dyed their hair and nails with henna, and also tinted the hands up to the wrist and that part of the foot covered by shoes. Muslim law required the removal of all body hair, and so both men and women removed hair from even the most intimate parts of the body. For this delicate procedure a very fine clay known as *ot* was applied to the body when it was moist from the sauna. It could not be left too long on the skin because it was an abrasive. The Koran prescribed that each person should perform this task for themselves, but the Ottoman ladies used their slaves to carry out this ritual service.

The seraglio slaves were certain that they possessed the secrets of beauty and used several creams and miraculous unguents, including the balm of Mecca, which was eagerly adopted by European women in the eighteenth century. Ladies in London and Paris moved heaven and earth and begged friends and traders travelling to the East to procure even a tiny jar of the precious cream which smoothed and rejuvenated the skin. Turkish women used make-up with great skill, whitening their faces and necks with a paste made from almonds and

BALM OF MECCA

As to the balm of Mecca, I will certainly send you some, but it is not as easily got as you suppose it, and I cannot, in consequence, advise you to make use of it. I know not how it comes to have such universal applause. All the ladies of my acquaintance at London and Vienna have begged me to send pots of it to them. I have had a present of a small quantity (which, I'll assure you, is very valuable) of the best sort and with great joy applied it to my face, expecting some wonderful effect to my advantage. The next morning the change indeed was wonderful; my face was swelled to a very extraordinary size, and all over as red as my Lady H—'s. It remained in this lamentable state three days, during which you may be sure I passed my time very ill. I believed it would never be otherwise; and, to my mortification, Mr Wortley reproached my indiscretion without ceasing. However, my face is since in *statu quo*; nay, I am told by the ladies here, that it is much mended by the operation, which I confess I cannot perceive in my looking-glass. Indeed, if one were to form an opinion of this balm from their faces, one should think very well of it. They all make use of it, and have the loveliest bloom in the world.

Lady Mary Wortley Montagu from a letter 'To the Lady Rich' from Belgrade Village, June 17, 1717

jasmine, tinting their eyelids, lengthening their eyebrows with China ink and painting beauty spots on their cheeks.

After the sauna the ladies dried themselves on soft towels and put on high wood and mother-of-pearl clogs to keep their feet dry and to avoid slipping on the wet marble floors. Then they went into the dressing room, a vast hall that was in effect a coffee house for the Turkish ladies. Here, sitting on cushions and sofas, they indulged in drinks and sorbets, nibbled fruit and snacks and, above all, gossiped – about the sultan's new favourite; or some scanty bits of news brought by a Jewish woman trader selling her wares; of what might be going on in the fascinating world beyond the Topkapí; or the secret vice of some important eunuch and about the concubines. Lesbianism was rampant. Unsatisfied by the rare pleasure they got from the sultan and acutely aware of their bodies, harem women had ardent sexual relationships with each other and even passionate love affairs, to the disgust of European men who attributed this, 'and many other dishonest practices' to the custom of frequenting the baths.

A *hamam* in the Dolmabahçe Palace, the nineteenth-century residence of the sultans. The Ottoman baths had three rooms: the entrance which was used for dressing and undressing; the *tepidarium* where the temperature was moderate; and the *calidarium* with fountains, seats and a central platform used for massage. In Turkish baths there were no tubs because of a superstition that stagnant water harboured evil spirits. Small basins filled with hot and cold water from the fountains were used to wash in. *Foggie diverse del vestire de' Turchi*, XV century. Venice, Biblioteca Nazionale Marciana.

THE LUXURIOUS NATURE OF THE TURKISH LIFESTYLE

In an apartment furnished with all the luxuries of the East, a sultana with translucent skin receives her lover with a smile that promises much. European lords travelling in the East had this fantasy and in secret dreamed of amorous adventures. Turkish women were considered lustful and ready to give themselves. Apparently beautiful and wild, freer than any other women in the world, they invited this sort of daydream. A mingling of the races had produced a great variety of beauty: tall, opulent matrons with large dark eyes and full lips; small, plump girls with rounded faces, noses, mouths and arms, with an expression of sweet resignation; and bold and self-possessed women with a spark of malice.

Turkish women, either on a whim or as a gesture of rebellion, sometimes showed a propensity to flirt, and might respond to the advances of an admirer with a smiling glance, or deliberately drop a flower or handkerchief for a suitor or gallant to pick up. Ottoman women were exuberant, and loved to be out in the world. According to De Amicis, he enjoyed a game of casually selecting one particular woman to 'follow her from a distance to see the ways in which she would manage to get every crumb of pleasure out of wandering along the street'.

This woman might be visiting a friend who lived on the other side of Istanbul, or shopping in the bazaar. Ladies would take a caique to the shop of a European merchant in Pera and then return down the Golden Horn, stopping at Eyüp for a quick prayer in the mosque or to eat an ice cream sitting on a tomb in the company of the dead, as is customary in the East where there is no great division between those that are alive and those that are dead. Lured on by the thousand and one pleasures of the capital, these Turkish women were like spinning tops, in perpetual movement.

Turkish women, with their beautiful and slightly savage looks, enchanted Westerners.
Raccolta di 120 stampe, Venetiis, 1783. Venice, Biblioteca Nazionale Marciana.

Their veil freed them totally, and with all the comings and goings even the most jealous husband would find it difficult it to try to discover what his wife was up to. Women in search of an adventure found their robes highly convenient and had no difficulty in buying the complicity of a Jewish merchant who would place the back room of his shop at her disposal for a tryst. Sometimes a high price was paid for this sort of intrepid behaviour, and in the cold morning light the naked and still warm body of a beautiful woman wrapped in a coarse *ferace*, might be found in a back alley of Pera. When this occurred, a summary inquest was set up by the government, who rarely discovered the identity of the victim; revenge was left to relatives if they were not prepared to settle the matter with money.

Turkish women not only enchanted men with their beauty, they bewitched them and claimed that they could govern the hearts and wills of others though magic. They employed love potions and had filtres of various kinds to remedy any possible problem. Such beliefs were widespread among women at every level of society. Even in the Imperial Harem, amazing tales were repeated of bewitchings or lovers made to vanish into thin air; the telling of horoscopes, cabbalism and necromancy flourished. Several princesses, for instance the nineteenth-century *valide* Pertevniyel, practised these arts of foretelling the future. In mysticism women sought relief from the tedious daily lives they led, hoping to use magic to condemn their enemies and advance the fortunes of those they loved.

In the House of Felicity love was complicated, even when not induced by artifice, and it was never private. The intricacies of Byzantine ceremonial found their way even into the bedrooms of the Princes of Altai, and the rough lovemaking of the steppes of Central Asia was replaced by soft Levantine intrigue. The Lords of the Bosporus no longer conquered, but issued orders, even in matters of love. When the sultan wanted to sleep with a woman he would communicate this wish to the supervisor of the harem. If he was not certain who to choose, the girls were politely paraded before the lord who took his time looking them over. A handkerchief thrown before the favoured one signalled his choice for the night. Preparations then began in the seraglio: the chosen girl was taken to the *hamam* and placed in the expert hands of its supervisor and her assistants. She was massaged, washed and perfumed, after which she was decked out in fine linen, clothed in a beautiful gown and adorned with jewels. A black eunuch escorted her to the private apartments of the sultan, who rarely went to the woman's room. All night the eunuchs kept guard outside the royal bedchamber. The light of the flickering torches would give the girl a glimpse of her master, already settled in bed. Words were superfluous, and absolute silence reigned, that silence which Easterners perceive to be the highest form of respect, far better than often indecorous words. The girl approached the foot of the imperial bed, lifted the coverlet with her forehead and advanced up the bed until she was face to face with the sultan of sultans. At this point etiquette was forgotten and the young girl would summon all the wiles and play the erotic games she had learned under the apprenticeship of the eunuchs or which she had practised in secret with another girl or even a still-intact eunuch.

'These women can sing, dance, laugh, entertain, invent a thousand amusements. They visit the homes of the newly appointed ambassadors, and attend weddings, baptisms and circumcisions. These women are not sluts who dance for money, but part of the Sultan's court…'.
George De La Chappelle, *Recuel de divers portraits*, Paris, 1648. Venice, Biblioteca Nazionale Marciana.

In the House of Felicity love was a complicated matter, and even when it functioned without artifice, it was never private. The Byzantine ceremony entered the bedroom of the Turkish princes and the soft Levantine lovemaking replaced the rough love games of the steppes.
Frederick Arthur Bridgman, *Odalisque*. London, Mathaf Gallery.

sultans. At this point etiquette was forgotten and the young girl would summon all the wiles and play the erotic games she had learned under the apprenticeship of the eunuchs or which she had practised in secret with another girl or even a still-intact eunuch.

In that first night of love the concubine gambled her entire life. A wrong move, a tiny mistake might disenchant the sultan for ever, but a successful encounter could lead

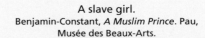

A slave girl.
Benjamin-Constant, *A Muslim Prince*. Pau, Musée des Beaux-Arts.

to further nights of amorous passion. The following morning the sultan would send the woman presents – robes, jewels or money – commensurate with his interest and the satisfaction received. Ottoman lords had hundreds of favourites in their harems and could choose a different courtesan every night. Rarely did they have a relationship with only one woman.

European travellers who wished to hear the most intimate details of life at the imperial court would bribe the eunuchs and Jewish women who peddled their wares there. They would pretend that they were familiar with what went on in the House of Felicity, but often turned out to be swindlers, simply greedy for money. The custom of choosing the night's companion with a handkerchief and the glide up the imperial bed have been repudiated as stories invented and passed on by European writers. Lady Wortley Montagu herself denied them, saying she had asked the widow of a sultan if they were true. True or false, in Ottoman circles ceremony always stood in place of words, and when the secrets of the soul or the wild fantasies of love were sought, Ottomans preferred to use symbols and gestures which allowed them to speak through a flower or the shade of a garment. But these too were secret, known only to Turks, who would never have revealed them to an infidel.

following pages
The favourite who had been chosen for the night was accompanied by a black eunuch to the sultan's apartment. Absolute silence reigned, and by the dim light of the torch the girl approached the foot of the bed and slowly slid forwards up the bed until she reached the head of her lord.
Jean-Auguste Ingres, *The Grand Odalisque*, 1814. Paris, Musée du Louvre.

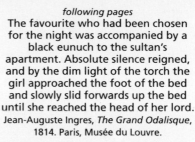

The music room of Sultan Selim III.
Istanbul, Aynalikavak.

PALACE ENTERTAINMENT

Many entertainments enlivened the Ottoman court. Music, dance, theatrical performances, games, tournaments, excursions and boat trips passed the time and gave pleasure. The sultan, the *valide* and the princesses sat on comfortable low divans in a pavilion or in the Hall of the Emperor, known as the *hünkâr sofasi*, arranged for the performances. They would watch the sensual and seductive movements of dancers dressed in close-fitting costumes which revealed everything as they moved to the rhythm of Eastern melodies, beating time with castanets.

Music, singing and dance were essential parts of a concubine's education. In all Ottoman harems girls who showed talent in these arts were tutored, usually by older women, who passed on their traditions. There was a huge choice of instruments to play: the harp, violin, various types of flute, drums, the *santur* or psaltery, the lute, lyre or *kanun*.

At the Topkapí there was a large orchestra, composed entirely of women. The earliest musical group at the Ottoman court was formed at the end of the fourteenth century by Sultan Beyazit I, known as 'The Lightning', and his wife, Olivera, a Serbian princess. The Turks loved music, which had also been important in the palaces of Byzantium, and once settled in Constantinople they cultivated this type of entertainment. Several sultans were good musicians and composers and promoted the art of music. Selim III, who ruled at the end of the eighteenth century, organized musicians and dance groups and put the well-known musician Sadullah in charge of instructing the odalisques.

The *köçek oyunu*, one of the favourite traditional dances, was performed by men in female attire. In the harem it was danced by the girls wearing the traditional *köçek* dress, a voluminous brocade skirt and a shirt worked in gold thread. Another popular dance was the *tavşan oyunu* for which black *şalvar* were worn and tight-fitting bodices. These vigorous dances required great skill. The dancers would cross their arms, jump and throw back their heads, fanning out their hair which hung in two loose strands. The dances were always a

Music was much appreciated at the Topkapí, which had a large female orchestra.
Costumi orientali, XVII century. Bologna, Biblioteca Comunale dell'Archiginnasio.

great success, and a Venetian diplomat who was lucky enough to witness a performance reported that the movements of the Turkish girls were so sensual as to 'make marble melt'.

As the court became more modern and opened up to Western culture, in particular that of France, the sultan imported musicians and dancing masters from Europe. The girls in the seraglio were taught new dances but still retained the rich traditions of Asia. The innovations brought some subversion to the palace, and when relationships began to develop between the teachers and their pupils that had little to do with music, the sultan insisted on collective lessons supervised by the black eunuchs.

facing page
Gustavo Simoni, *Court Musicians*.
London, Mathaf Gallery.

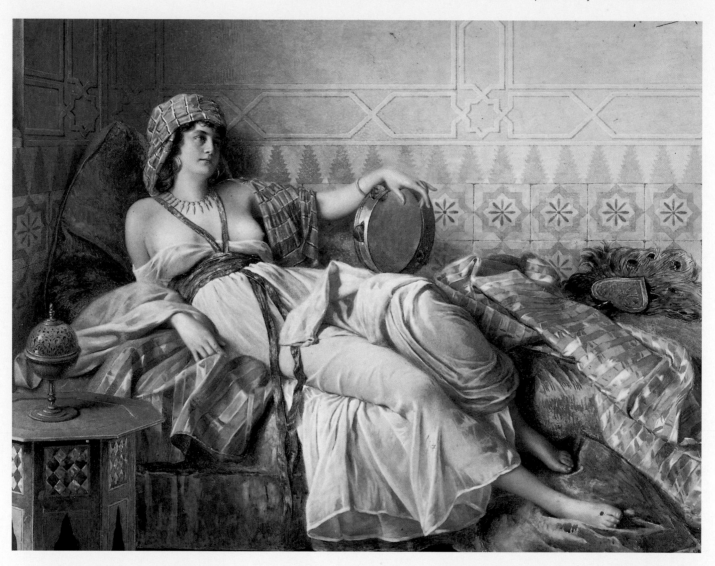

Those girls in the harem who showed an aptitude for music were given instruction by elderly teachers who passed on musical traditions. There was a wide choice of instruments such as the harp, the violin, the drums, the psaltery and the lyre.
Francesco Ballesio, *The Musician*. Paris, Nataf Galerie.

In the nineteenth century, Western music was favoured at court and, with the exception of Mahmut II who loved the traditional lyric poems, the sultans surrounded themselves with foreign artists. It was at this time that the vogue started for Turkish tunes arranged as marches, such as those composed by Donizetti's brother, who had been summoned to Istanbul by Abdül Mecit to direct the imperial orchestra. Drums and flutes were dominant, satisfying Turkish taste without offending European sensibilities. The ladies of the harem began to study the piano and the melodies of French songs began to disturb the silence of the Dolmabahçe Palace, where the court now resided.

Performances were almost always in the hands of the women. From time to time, however, Turkish and foreign artists, musicians, actors and mimes were invited to give performances of avant-garde pieces. In Turkey, the only theatre was the primitive and

simple *karagöz*, a shadow show with clever caricatures of typical Turks. Its repertory was a series of burlesques based on misunderstandings and puns. The tales were salacious and the exploits of the characters were recounted with gusto. The *karagöz* was often performed in the seraglio, where the women, seated on a platform, watched spectacles that were so liberal as to scandalize many Europeans. French and Italian companies were invited to give performances, but an Ottoman company was formed only in the nineteenth century, under the direction of an Armenian woman.

Among the games preferred by the Lords of the Bosporus were jousts, which reminded them of the freedom of their nomadic past. The sultan, with his ladies, delighted in watching the tournaments organized by pages and officers in the great courtyards of the Topkapí. There was the *cirid*, a tournament in which young men on Arab horses jousted, armed with javelins without blades. The knights either attacked or tried to avoid their adversaries, describing huge circles, galloping swiftly or backing off with great skill. In this way they avoided the javelin or caught it in mid-flight. If it fell to the ground, they would scoop it up without dismounting using a hook attached to their saddlebow. Other games included the *tomak*, a competition between two teams using a wooden ball attached to a rope, and wrestling naked to the waist and greased with oil.

In their games, Turks dressed in flaming colours, would race on foot and on horseback, showing great skill and prowess. They also took part in trials of strength: splitting rocks on their chests; competing in strong-arm contests; shattering bronze clubs with their fists; carrying heavy wooden columns on their heads, and balancing up to nine men on their shoulders. Women tended to prefer the acrobats who performed the most dangerous feats with astonishing agility.

In their jousts the horsemen attacked or sought to avoid their opponents, riding their horses hard to avoid a javelin or catching it in the air. If they missed, they did not dismount, but retrieved the javelin with a hook attached to their saddle.
Giulio Ferrario, *Il Costume antico e moderno*, Milan, 1828. Venice, Biblioteca Nazionale Marciana.

Fights between animals and performances by tamed animals were popular, especially those using elephants and bears trained to dance to the music of drums. The delicate concubines would be simultaneously fascinated and terrified by the bellowing of the wild animals in the sultan's zoo. According to Bassano, the animals were kept under the Hippodrome in a building the Byzantines used as a cistern; here they were chained sufficiently far apart so as to be unable to devour each other. He mentioned lions and lionesses, lynx, leopards and wild cats, bears, boars, badgers, elephants, giraffes and claimed that there was a wild man, although he never succeeded in seeing him.

The women of the harem on the whole preferred less boisterous entertainment than these dangerous games and frightening spectacles. When they were not occupied in entertaining the sultan, they often played checkers and tric trac, a sort of backgammon; card games, which were introduced during the reign of Mehmet V were also popular. The pastimes of the young girls were fairly simple: they enjoyed dressing up as men, mimicking the sultan and eunuchs and splashing each other in the pool. Their games resembled those of children rather than adults, but their average age was only seventeen and the sheltered and narrow life they led preserved an ingenuous and childlike nature.

Deriving from their origins on the steppes, the Ottoman Turks maintained a strong link with nature. They loved trees, flowers, water, life in the open air and never really became accustomed to indoor life and confined spaces. At the Imperial Palace, time was spent as much as possible in the kiosks surrounded by greenery, and the sultan rejoiced in his wonderful gardens, both big and small, with their exotic flowers and old trees. Whenever he wanted to promenade with his ladies, the word *halvet*, or 'retreat', was intoned in a loud voice and immediately everyone would

Ottoman dignitaries enjoying the game of *tomak*, a team-game played with a ball attached to a string.
Giulio Ferrario, *Il Costume antico e moderno*, Milan, 1828. Venice, Biblioteca Nazionale Marciana.

withdraw, clearing the way and allowing the royal party to wander freely. Excitement was intense when the great lord decided to organize a trip on his brigantine or an expedition outside the palace. The girls vied in dressing up, and awaited the moment of departure with impatience. The sense of anticipation affected the eunuchs as well, since they were responsible for the observation of innumerable court regulations. In the event of a trip by sea, the heavily veiled women were accompanied to the pier where the boats waited. They could only glimpse the world outside through the lattice windows that hid them from public view. For a trip to the country, the girls entered their carriages at the harem door, and servants cleared away all curious onlookers in the streets so that no one might dare to look at them.

The many lovely walks within the walls of the overcrowded city of Constantinople were matched by gardens with flowing water and abundant flowers and trees on the outskirts of the city. The landscaped gardens of the Sweet Waters of Europe at the narrow end of the Golden Horn, with their harmonious arrangement of plants and limpid streams, were set out among the hills. Small waterfalls flowed from a canal and there was a kiosk for the sultan's pleasure. When Turkey was seized by French fashion in the eighteenth century, the sultan had the pavilion enlarged and redecorated, and the canal was transformed into a copy of that at Fontainebleau. The women of the seraglio were enchanted by this innovation as it gave them a freedom previously unknown. The canal was extended and the place, known as *Kagithane*, was given a French name. The girls of the harem often came here and while the women walked among the marble fountains and over the little bridges, the sultan enjoyed the coolness of the waters, eventually falling asleep by the murmuring waterfalls.

For longer trips the Bosporus would be chosen. The straits 'in which a god flows', were like a river that emptied the stormy waters of the Black Sea and meandered through the soft hills covered in vegetation. In spring, when the Judas trees and the

preceding pages
The ladies preferred more tranquil pastimes such as chess and card games to the more boisterous forms of entertainment. Their amusements were more childlike, in keeping with their tender age and sheltered upbringing.
Jean-Baptist Huysmans, *The Juggler*. London, Mathaf Gallery.

When the great lord gave his permission for a boat trip to be organized, a wave of excitement would sweep through the harem. The girls competed in their toilettes and the thrill of anticipation would spread to the eunuchs who still had to ensure that the almost infinite number of rules regulating court life were respected.
Turchia Album di 62 foto, n.d. Venice, Biblioteca Nazionale Marciana.

51. *La tour de Leandre.*   P. Séb

bougainvillea covered the land with dazzling colour, the banks of this 'river' were a delight. Autumn was also enchanting, with yellows and browns highlighted with every possible shade of red.

Along these straits the sultans, prominent citizens and rich Europeans built large wooden houses facing the water, complete with jetties. In these lovely residences, surrounded by nature, the sultans spent increasing time escaping the heat and the terrible epidemics that often devastated the city and rejoicing in the sweetness of their leisure. This stretch of water was always crowded with caiques, but all the boats dispersed at once or hastened to pull to the shore when the sultan's brigantine approached.

Sometimes the sultan allowed an inland excursion to be organized from the summer palaces. One of the favourite destinations to the north was the Belgrade forest, a valley scattered with kiosks, shaded by pomegranates, willows, plane and almond trees and filled with melodious birdsong. The air was heavy with the perfume of roses, lilies and narcissi. This area, which had been popular since Byzantine times, was developed by Süleyman the Magnificent, who had a village built on the old city of Petra and peopled it with Serbian prisoners from the recently conquered Belgrade, which gave its name to the new settlement. The place became a favourite resort of the rich citizens of Istanbul who spent their summers there among the beeches, oaks, pines, elms and poplars of the only forest in Thrace.

Groups of women would visit such naturally beautiful places accompanied by their slaves. If they included ladies from the seraglio, everyone they encountered would leave, since no indiscreet glance was allowed to fall on a girl whose veil might have slipped accidentally to her shoulders, leaving her face uncovered, in the excitement of an innocent game with her companions. The eunuchs kept a close watch on this Eden at all times, while the great lord looked on, amused by the gaiety of his concubines.

Shopping was a favourite diversion. When court regulations were severe during the golden age, the ladies were not free to go out and merchants came to the court. They were trusted dealers who dealt exclusively with the chief of the black eunuchs and left their goods with him. Jewish women also did business after receiving special permission to enter the harem to sell their wares. This trade was very lucrative

The Bosporus was a favourite venue for a trip in caiques. These narrow straights between the Sea of Marmara and Black Sea are flanked by rounded hills rich in vegetation and lined with lovely wooden houses.
Foggie diverse del vestire de' Turchi, XV century. Venice, Biblioteca Nazionale Marciana.

because the sultanas did not have to worry about expense and in any case had no way of verifying the value of what they were buying. When harem etiquette relaxed, the sultanas began to venture out to the elegant shops of Istanbul to buy all sorts of trinkets.

Rich and abundant Istanbul offered a thousand temptations. At this cross-roads between East and West could be found jewellery from Turkey and Europe; precious fabrics made in Venice and Bursa; Murano mirrors; clocks studded with precious stones; elegant hats and eagerly sought-after French perfumes. Wrapped in their colourful *ferace* the ladies admired, discarded, and would finally choose a wide range of articles. They were served by unctuous merchants who afforded them every courtesy, while the carriages with the imperial insignia waited at the door guarded by fierce-looking eunuchs. Women could spend a fortune in an afternoon, but this was common in the East. If high-ranking ladies were allowed to lead a life of uninterrupted pleasure, of excursions, baths, amusements and new fashions, and if husbands who demanded a little economy were considered mad, to what might the ladies of the seraglio, those beloved women of the 'Sultan of Sultans, the Shadow of God on Earth' not feel themselves entitled?

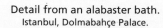

Detail from an alabaster bath.
Istanbul, Dolmabahçe Palace.

Within the city walls, Constantinople was overcrowded, but the environs of the city were enchanting with lovely gardens, well watered and rich in flowers and trees. Turks loved the open air and would visit the surrounding countryside in groups.
Pietro Bellò, *On the Road to Istanbul*, 1909. Bassano del Grappa, Pinacoteca.

following pages
Ottoman culture showed a deep respect and devotion for the mother, who in every family was the indisputable head of the women's quarters in which lived daughters, daughters-in-law, female servants and sons up to a certain age.
Frederick Goodall, *A New Light in the Harem*. Liverpool, Sudley Art Gallery.

Life at court was measured by a great number of official engagements conducted according to the complex ceremonies so customary in Asia. The birth of the sultan's children, the circumcision of the young princes, military victories and religious feasts were rigorously observed and celebrated.

The arrival of a child was a very important event. A midwife, with the aid of experienced older women, assisted the mother in labour. To help a woman bear the pain of childbirth, women musicians were summoned. Once a child was born, a long string of formalities was observed. The chief of the black eunuchs announced the news to the sultan and the court; the cannon by the Topkapí Gate fired seven salvoes for the birth of a male, three for a female. The announcement was repeated five times in twenty-four hours, and each section of the palace celebrated the event with the sacrifice of five rams if the new-born were a boy, three if it were a girl. The population of Istanbul and that of the whole Empire, informed of the event by town criers and an imperial edict, participated by gathering in the mosques and making merry in the streets.

A few days after having given birth, the mother took possession of a magnificently furnished pavilion. The bed was adorned with a red satin cover, embroidered with precious stones such as rubies, emeralds and pearls. It was here that the mother and the newborn baby received the visits of those who came to pay their respects, and this continued for about six days. The mistress of ceremonies in the harem, the *saray usta*, informed the other sultanas and the wives of Ottoman dignitaries of the happy event. The ladies who had been invited to the palace gathered at the residence of the grand vizier's wife and were taken together in a carriage to the harem. When they arrived at the new mother's room they offered their congratulations by kissing the hem of her coverlet and seated themselves on the sofas. A little later the sultanas entered with the other ladies of the court and, in their turn, presented the required congratulations. Then, as etiquette demanded, they took the seat of honour on a raised platform situated in front of the bed so as not to mix with the other women. During this ceremony two young girls held back the bed curtains. The midwife and the wet-nurse sat at the foot of the bed, the latter holding the child in her arms. Both were highly respected and received gifts at the birth of the baby and often maintained ties of affection with the princes and princesses for the rest of their lives.

The Topkapí was ablaze with light in the event of a birth and in the harem the slaves sang sweet songs, danced and improvised pantomimes. An atmosphere of general rejoicing pervaded the seraglio, even though it may have not been shared equally by all the women, since each birth caused

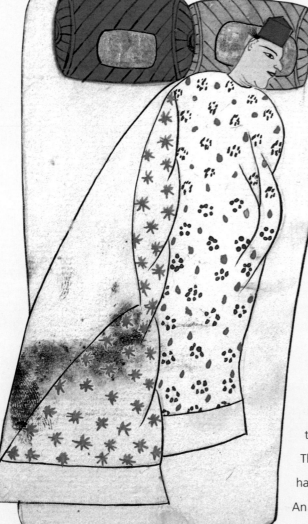

The great event of maternity represented in its various phases: a pregnant woman, the birth, the mother and child. Childbirth was an event controlled by women. The woman giving birth was assisted by a midwife and elderly women, and musicians played to help her bear the pangs of childbirth.
Costumi orientali, XVII century. Bologna, Biblioteca Comunale dell'Archiginnasio.

a shift in the delicate balance of the harem and brought with it inevitable jealousies and hatreds. On the sixth day, a new cradle was escorted to the palace accompanied by an imposing host of ministers and court officials. This precious object, studded with jewels and adorned with feathers in the case of a prince, was handed over to the chief black eunuch, who carried it into the harem. He gave it to the mistress of ceremonies, who then saw to its transportation into the room of the newly delivered mother.

Upon the arrival of the cradle, all the women rose to their feet and the mother was the first to drop a handful of gold coins into the little bed. All the women copied this gesture to wish the baby well, and, with prayers and wishes for prosperity, the midwife gently placed the child in the cradle, rocked it three times, then took the child in her arms again while the lady guests covered the bed with richly embroidered materials. After the ceremony, slave girls served fruit, sorbets and sweet cakes. The following day the guests left the seraglio having bestowed their gifts on the mother, the child, and the mistress of ceremonies who had looked after them during their stay in the harem. Once the celebrations for the birth were over, the pavilion was cleared, and the mother and child moved out. Both were now embarked upon a journey which, if favoured by good fortune, might lead them to the highest peaks of the Ottoman Empire.

Another significant event was the circumcision of the sultan's sons. The celebrations could last thirty or forty days and here too a careful set of rules governed even the most insignificant details. Since diplomats from both Asia and Europe were present, the event became a display of Turkish power and wealth. Eye-witnesses at this demonstration could be counted upon to broadcast the wonders of the great lord's court far and wide.

The square in front of the Hippodrome was usually chosen as a venue for the celebrations, since it could hold vast numbers of people. In this huge space kitchens and pavilions were erected to house the foreign delegations, who were provided with every comfort for their stay both by day and overnight. A special platform was reserved for the sultan and high-ranking persons, while another, enclosed and provided with latticed windows, was reserved for the ladies and girl slaves of the great lord. Standing in perfect silence, the people awaited the arrival of the monarch, who would make his entrance like a god, seated in majesty on an Arab horse decked out with precious jewels.

Pietro Zen, a Venetian orator who was

facing page
**Commemoration of the birth of the
Prophet Mohammed (The Feast of
Mevlud) celebrated in the splendid
Blue Mosque of Sultan Ahmet.**
Giulio Ferrario, *Il Costume antico e moderno*,
Milan, 1828. Venice, Biblioteca
Nazionale Marciana.

present at the celebrations for the circumcision of the sons of Süleyman in June 1530, told of all sorts of events that took place one after the other. There were processions of the various military and professional orders, displays of skill and strength, tournaments and exhibitions of exotic animals, but most spectacular were the displays of fireworks at which the Turks excelled. For these, they created structures of all types, including towers, cities, castles and animals; on this occasion, a huge serpent was constructed. The fireworks were let off at night and the effect was sensational. Only after many days of celebration did the sons of the sultan make their solemn appearance. Mustafa, Mohammed and Selim proceeded from the old seraglio, where they had lived with their mothers and the other women and, escorted by the eunuchs and a cortège of courtiers, entered the Hippodrome on horseback. The first was dressed in crimson, the second in red satin, the third in gold brocade. Each carried a sword. Their skin was so white and their appearance so beautiful that even to Pietro Zen, not usually given to excessive tenderness, they seemed 'angels come down from Heaven'.

The circumcision took a few minutes and was carried out by a specialized barber who employed a sharpened razor. The wound was cauterized by very primitive methods. Bassano wrote that a powder to alleviate the pain was used, but most probably it was only wood ash. During these celebrations it was customary for others outside the court to have their own sons circumcised as well, and the imperial kitchens saw to the provision of abundant food not only for the guests of honour, but for the entire populace. In this manner even the poorest people could celebrate properly the circumcision of their own sons and feel that they were an integral part of the state, one that neither recognized or rewarded individualism.

On these occasions, eminent dignitaries sent gifts and *nahil*, decorations in the form of objects such as trees, animals and wonderful flowers made in wax by specialized craftsmen, which were often enriched by silver threads and precious stones. Like the

**Muslim boys on the day of their
circumcision. The animals that were to
be sacrificed during the ceremony
were also dressed up.**
Giulio Ferrario, *Il Costume antico e moderno*,
Milan, 1828. Venice, Biblioteca
Nazionale Marciana.

creations in sugar that adorned the tables of Europe, these *nahil* decorated the banquet tables, and the very large ones were carried there in procession.

The imperial ladies assisted at the public celebrations from a platform enclosed by a grille. Even set apart in this way, they could follow all the stages of this important occasion, watch with pride and trepidation the solemn entrance of their sons, peep at the pavilion in which the foreign princes were accommodated and enjoy the spectacle of the tumblers and the fireworks.

Military victories were celebrated with similar solemnity in the Ottoman Empire. The end of a campaign was greeted with general rejoicing by the people and was announced with great ostentation to friendly powers, who participated in the triumph of the great lord by sending gifts and delegations.

In Asia the measurement of time was different from that in Europe, and in the Turkish calendar, which followed the ancient Persian usage, the new year began on 21 March. This was known as the *Nevruz*, the beginning of spring, and was an occasion for merrymaking. Presents were exchanged, the sultan sent precious gifts to his favourites and spent the day with his ladies in the gardens of the palace. The rest of the Muslim year was marked by days of religious obligation set aside for religious observance and for social gatherings.

One of the most important of these was the period of fasting observed during *Ramadan*. Every Muslim who had reached the age of fourteen years was obliged to undertake this harsh penance, and in the Imperial Palace, as in every other Turkish home, solemn preparations were made for the ritual of purification. The first night of *Ramadan* was spent in prayer, and during the day a theologian gave a sermon in the harem. Abstinence lasted from dawn till sunset, and the end of the *iftar*, or fast, was announced by a roll of drums. At that hour the sultan invited his guests to share his evening meal. The ladies of the harem invited the wives of noblemen to eat with

The grand vizier receiving foreign ambassadors.
Giulio Ferrario, *Il Costume antico e moderno*, Milan, 1828. Venice, Biblioteca Nazionale Marciana.

them, while listening to songs and recitations. The end of *Ramadan* was marked by the *Şeker Bayramí,* the Sugar Festival. During these three days of celebrations the sultan visited the harem, distributed gifts and, amid general merrymaking, everyone feasted on sweets and drinks.

Islam imposes on all the Faithful the same duties and the obligation to fast, which for once places the rich and the poor on the same level, but even for this event the imperial family had certain privileges. Once a year the veneration of the Holy Relics housed in the palace took place. The ladies, dressed in restrained fashion and with their faces veiled, lined up before the door of the pavilion and slowly filed past the relics to kiss them. The sultan presented each woman with a handkerchief on which verses of the Koran had been embroidered, and after the ceremony a lunch was held. This custom was retained even after the court moved to the Dolmabahçe Palace, when a long procession of covered carriages transported the ladies of the harem from the Bosporus to the centre of Istanbul to take part in the traditional ceremony. The sultan and his ladies celebrated together the birth of the Prophet, when prayers were recited as well as poems recalling this event. After this, as usual, cakes and sorbets would be served.

An important feast day was the *Kurban Bayramí,* or Feast of the Sacrifice, in which every head of household had to sacrifice a ram, slaughtering it according to a fixed ritual. The sultan and well-to-do families donated the meat to the poor. Everyone poured out into the streets to enjoy a variety of entertainments. The members of the harem also celebrated by exchanging greetings and presents and received a visit from the sultan with all due solemnity. One of the rituals the women particularly enjoyed was the Friday parade to accompany the sultan to the mosque. On most occasions the ladies were obliged to celebrate ceremonial occasions in the solitude of their splendid harem or, if they were lucky, they might catch a glimpse of the public

The splendid valley of the Sweet Waters of Europe, a favourite spot of the Ottoman sultans.
Ignaz Mellin, *Voyage pittoresque de Constantinople et du Bosphore*, Paris, 1819. Parma, Biblioteca Palatina.

proceedings from behind the shutters of a narrow corridor that ran above the Imperial Gate of the Topkapí. But on the occasion of the Friday parade, they occupied an official position at the most exclusive level. The custom for the sultan to proceed with great pomp to the mosque and offer prayers in public was not merely an act of piety, but a political manifestation of great importance. Alone and in public he gave proof that he was alive, dispelled suspicions of assassination and plots against his life and assured the stability of the Empire. These ploys became more and more essential as the political position of the Ottomans became progressively more precarious.

Throughout the sixteenth century, Friday prayers took place in the basilica of Hagia Sophia which had been converted into a mosque. In the sixteenth century the lovely Blue Mosque, which had been built on the side of the Hippodrome as a rival to the Byzantine sanctuary, began to be used instead, while in the nineteenth century the sultan visited a different mosque each week. Along the short route from the palace to the place of prayer, a procession of the elite of the Empire could be observed. The grand vizier and other top ministers, pashas and high-ranking army and naval officers proudly dominated the crowd from the height of their glorious steeds. The sultan, accompanied by his black slaves, rode a magnificent Arab stallion caparisoned in jewels. As Eastern etiquette required in this country of absolute power, he made his way with exasperating slowness, the hieratical impersonation of a god, majestic and awesome, a fixed look in his eyes, which seemed to see nothing.

The ladies followed closely behind the sultan. First the queen mother, followed by the wives and then the favourites, and they, too, provided no less an imposing sight than their lord. Once in the mosque, they observed proceedings from a special platform discreetly surrounded by fine screens, never mingling with other people. Every Friday, come rain or shine, not only the populace but every foreigner in Constantinople flocked to the mosque and the route leading to it in a flurry of excitement to see the parade of the sultan and his concubines. European men and women avidly sought to catch every detail of that strange upside down world which frightened as well as fascinated them.

facing page
The Friday prayers at the Ortaköy Mosque with the sultan's guard lined up in front of the covered boats in which the women were transported from the harem. *Below*, **the interior of Hagia Sophia.**
Turchia Album di 62 foto, n.d., Venice, Biblioteca Nazionale Marciana.

The gardens of the seraglio in Constantinople.
Antonio Baratta, *Costantinopoli effigiata e descritta*, Turin, 1840. Venice, Biblioteca Nazionale Marciana.

Intérieur de la mosquée S:te Sophie.

THE EMPIRE OF THE WOMEN

In Ottoman society, in contrast to that of other Muslim states, women enjoyed a certain autonomy. They had recourse to the courts of justice, were permitted to own wealth and estates and to hold power.
Eugène Giraud, *Lord of the Harem*. London, Mathaf Gallery.

THE GREAT LORD AND HIS WIVES:
PERSONAL INFLUENCE AND POLITICAL POWER

In Ottoman society, unlike in other Muslim states, women held a remarkable position. They were allowed to own property and wealth, and could have recourse to justice when this was necessary. Turkish history provides examples of several high-class women who enjoyed power and freedom of movement.

The sultanas were shrewd, clever, farsighted and almost always endowed with a strong personality. They were often more intelligent than their consorts and well versed in public office. The lives of these women were dangerous, and a tough apprenticeship taught them to struggle and contend with solitude, enmity and

In the empire every individual could join the ruling class irrespective of ethnic origin or class, since what counted was ability, loyalty to the sultan and acceptance of the faith of Islam. The First Secretary of State. *Raccolta di 120 stampe*, Venetiis, 1783. Venice, Biblioteca Nazionale Marciana.

intrigue. Stiff competition weeded out many victims, and the woman who won through was well prepared to face any adversity in life. In the harem the women learned the art of exercising authority, while in the Topkapí, the sultans allowed themselves to succumb to a narrow and dissolute life. This state of affairs brought new characters to the fore, and encouraged and facilitated a reversal of roles.

Women's history during the time of the Ottoman Empire, so rich in fascinating events, followed the changes and developments of this complex society. Women are scarcely evident in the heroic age of the Empire, a tumultuous era during which the Knights of Altai installed themselves on the throne of Byzantium in 1453. European and Turkish princesses of those times were often rich and fascinating characters, but they were kept in the wings of a stage on which a play, already too encumbered with towering personalities, was being performed.

The Turkish Empire that took its place in Asia Minor was essentially a military state, tending towards conquest and expansion. There were two important elements in the political situation of the time: the many independent and rebellious aristocratic Turkish tribes and the feebleness of the Byzantines, whose territory they were about to occupy. In order to govern, the early sultans had to subjugate these two enemies, or at least bring them under control.

The Ottomans were primarily warriors, but not lacking in pragmatism. They employed alternately war and alliances. Abetted by the law of Islam, which allows four legal wives, the sultans made full use of matrimony for political ends. To control the Anatolian aristocracy, they married Turkoman women, but also, despite the seesaw relationship of alternating enmity and alliance, they contracted marriages of convenience with Byzantine princesses. The refined Greek emperors, overcoming their disgust for the barbarians from the steppes, gave their daughters to the sultans in the erroneous belief that these links with the new masters might stem the ineluctable flow of events.

It seems that the first marriage between an Ottoman prince and a Christian woman was that of Orhan Gazi (1324–62) and Lülüfer or Nilüfer, the daughter of the Christian governor of Yarhisar, a city lying between Bursa and Eskişehir. The scanty records inform us that she was seventeen in 1298, when she married the future *gazi* of the Turks who was then eleven years of age and not yet sultan. The Turkish name by which the girl is known was given to her after her marriage, a custom which was kept right up to the fall of the Empire, underlining the new life that began at court. When he mounted the throne and began to acquire influence, Orhan sealed this alliance with a new union. In 1346 he married Theodora, daughter of the Byzantine co-emperor John V Cantacuzenus, and the marriage was celebrated with such pomp as to merit a mention in the chronicles of the time. From the first marriage were born Süleyman and the hereditary prince Murat I, who in turn married Helena Cantacuzenus.

Throughout the fourteenth century, the marriages of the princes were dictated by reasons of state. But the new political trend introduced by Murat I (1362–89) and Beyazit I (1389–1403) brought many changes in the course of one century, which also affected 'the matters of the heart'. The sultans freed themselves from the powerful Turkish aristocracy and inaugurated the practice known as *devşirme*, a system of forced recruitment among the Christians, which, when it was later applied on a large scale, revolutionized the structure of society, the formation of the social classes and the very concepts of ethnicity and nobility.

Sultan Beyazit I did not enjoy the fruits of his innovations and, following the practices of his predecessors, formed several marriages of convenience. Looking down the list of the wives he chose, one can easily perceive the direction that Turkish politics was taking. Beyazit was a forceful personality, a man of swift decisions as his nickname of *Yildirim*, 'The Lightning', testifies. He married Fülane, the daughter of the king of the Bulgars, then two Turkoman princesses, Devletşah Germiyanoğlu and Fülane Karamanoğlu and finally Olivera, daughter of the Serbian king, who brought a Christian influence to the court. His successor Murat II (1421–51) also married a Serbian princess, Maria Olivera, a woman with political acumen and farsighted enough to advise her husband to pursue a policy of peace when the Christian crusade against the Turks, ordered by the Pope in 1443, was initially successful. The Christians were finally routed at Varna in 1444.

Sultan Mehmet II was stubborn and authoritarian, a secretive man without pity. He was the conqueror of Constantinople, appreciative of Greek culture and a lover of art.
Foggie diverse del vestire de' Turchi, XV century. Venice, Biblioteca Nazionale Marciana.

A precious scimitar. The safety of the
Empire was not entrusted to the
number of fortresses but to disciplined
soldiers who fought selflessly and with
energy. The sultans themselves were
warriors above all else, and up to the
sixteenth century they personally led
their troops into battle.
Istanbul, Topkapí.

In the crucial years of the formation of the Empire, Christian princesses played an important role. The environment into which they married was well disposed towards innovation. Here, the Islamic faith, which had formally been accepted, coexisted with the mystical fantasies of shamanism, and many of the princesses remained Christians, having their children secretly baptised. Thanks to the vast entourage they brought with them, they introduced at court their own culture and lifestyle, both of which would eventually transform this tribal society into an organized state.

With the conquest in 1453 of Constantinople, symbol of refined Byzantine culture, Sultan Mehmet II consolidated the structure of the Ottoman Empire. As a result of his prestigious victory, he could conclude the process of the centralization of power and, having deprived the nobles of their power and confiscated their estates, he placed his slaves recruited through the *devşirme* in key positions in government.

This sultan had ten women. The origins and date of birth of Gülbahar, 'Rose of Spring', is uncertain, but possibly she was born around the year 1434, though the date of her entry into the imperial harem, 1446, is known. Two years later the heir to the throne, Beyazit II, was born, and the sultana died in 1492. She was followed by a Serbian lady who is believed to have been related to the Hungarian sovereign Matthias Corvinus. Then came three Turkoman princesses from eastern Anatolia. Mehmet not only took over what was left of Byzantium and its eastern colonies but also the last survivors of that doomed empire in the persons of Helena, daughter of Demitrios Palaeologus, Anna, the daughter of David Comnenus, Emperor of Trebizond, and Irene Cantacuzenus. Fülane came from the noble Genovese family of the Gattilusi, feudal lords of Lemnos, Thasos and other Byzantine lands, which were rapidly disintegrating in the aftermath of the Ottoman victory.

The authoritarian Mehmet also abolished matrimony and separated the harem from the imperial residence and the seat of power. The time of alliances and arrangements and political settlements was over, and the Knights of Altai would not be dominated, even in matters of the heart, and no longer sought to have consorts.

But history defeated the conquerors of Constantinople. Their women, after a long apprenticeship in slavery, learned not to be faithful and submissive slaves, but human beings, free to act, to think and to love.

THE GOLDEN ERA OF THE OTTOMAN PORTE

Once the court was installed at Istanbul, the harem acquired a prestigious role in the conduct of matters of state. The characters of the women became more definite and personalities emerged. Their activities were recorded and the list of public works undertaken and paid for by women became extensive.

In the second half of the fifteenth century, marked by the civil war between the sons of Mehmet, two of the sultan's favourites stand out: Gülbahar and Çiçek Hatun. Gülbahar, the mother of Beyazit II (1481–1512), was a wise and experienced advisor. Çiçek, the mother of Cem, was a courageous and resolute woman who gave support to her son in his unfortunate military campaigns.

These women had lived for many years side by side in the seraglio, but fate had ordained them to be bitter enemies, engaged in a battle for which there could be but one winner. The cautious Beyazit reaped the triumph, and fortune smiled on his mother Gülbahar, who was honoured as first lady of the Empire in the magnificent Ottoman capital. The fate of Çiçek Hatun was very different; she passed her remaining years in bitter exile in Cairo, able to follow the peregrinations of her son in Europe only through letters.

The sixteenth century was the golden age of the Ottoman Porte. It opened with the reign of Selim I (1512–20), a resolute and solitary man, with little inclination towards luxury and pleasure. Nicknamed *Yavuz*, 'The Grim', he was an excellent military leader, given to drastic solutions and excessive measures. Before he mounted the throne of Osman, Selim had lived for a long time in Trebizond, the ancient capital of the Comneni, where he met and joined with the beautiful and intelligent Hafsa Hatun, the daughter of Mengli Giray, the khan of Crimea. The princess, in whose veins ran the blood of Genghis Khan, was about fifteen years old when she gave birth to Süleyman 1494. In the years that she spent in Trebizond she distinguished herself as a patron and instigator of numerous charitable activities, including the construction of hospitals, schools and mosques.

Once established in the capital, Hafsa Hatun entered the political scene with great passion. In her powerful role of sultana mother, she took an active part in the rise of Ibrahim, a slave

Beyazit II, The Saint, and his successor Selim I the Grim (on the right), two capable and determined sultans but with very different characters. The former was a cautious man who deferred to his mother, the latter inclined towards luxury and the harem. Codice Cicogna, *Memorie turchesche, XVII century*. Venice, Biblioteca del Museo Correr.

of Christian origins, who was to become grand vizier. She also laid the foundations for a system of favouritism, which in the subsequent century became palace factionalism. This princess, so quiet in appearance but implacable underneath, surreptitiously initiated the epoch of influential sultanas. Their decisions became important in the conduct of government, the parties they created became political pressure groups, and slowly but surely they started to erode the power of the most absolute sovereign of the world until they shattered it into a thousand splinters.

The long reign of Süleyman the Magnificent (1520–66) marked the peak of imperial splendour. The Ottoman Empire was a vast state for the times, in which many peoples of diverse race, language and religion lived together in peace. Huge economic resources allowed an extremely efficient military structure to be maintained, and liberal patronage of the arts gave rise to artistic inspiration and the construction of valuable monuments.

Süleyman had many qualities, as was recognized by historians. He maintained the warlike tradition of the *gazi* and became at the same time a shrewd statesman and a wise administrator. In his reforms he was as much concerned with social and personal relationships and the mechanisms of power as he was with administrative reforms. A strong but just monarch, and the best-loved of the Ottoman sultans, he gathered around him a group of people who greatly influenced his decisions. These were his mother, Hafsa, his wife, Hürrem or Roxelana, his daughter, Mihrimah, Grand Vizier Ibrahim, and the Venetian Alvise Gritti, all his cherished counsellors.

Although he had several favourites, among whom was Gülbahar (1499–81), the mother of the heir-apparent Mustafa, Süleyman formed an alliance with Roxelana. This beautiful slave managed to secure her union with the young sultan by giving him six children in the space of ten years. The eldest was Mehmet, a liberal and humanitarian

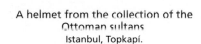

A helmet from the collection of the
Ottoman sultans
Istanbul, Topkapi.

prince who died at an early age. He was his father's favourite, and much beloved by his subjects, and in his grief at the boy's death Süleyman had a great number of slaves set free. Then there was Mihrimah, a woman born to be happy, loved without reserve by both her mother and father; Abdullah, who died a few months after he was born; Selim, born in 1524, the future sultan, cruel and violent, a slave to his passion for wine; and Beyazit, a peaceful boy, the complete opposite of his brother Selim. Contemporary observers saw him as a supporter of his step-brother Mustafa. The last son, born in 1531, was the vivacious, lively and ironic Cihangir who never held any government position because of a physical defect, but who lived in great contentment with his father.

The art of calligraphy was revered by Islam since it preserved the words of the Creator through the message of the Prophet. It reached its perfect form during the Ottoman Empire. It was not only employed in manuscripts but as decoration for portals and the *timpani* of mosques and palaces.
Istanbul, Topkapí.

Süleyman, though an able statesman, tended to rely excessively on a few favourites. The first of these was Ibrahim Pasha, elected grand vizier in 1523, who had been a slave, captured in Parga and brought up at court. The sultan saw him as a trustworthy friend, and he was the first man from the *devşirme* to be elected to such high office. Roxelana approved of his appointment since his advice had contributed to the denigration of the former Grand Vizier Piri Mehmet, a member of the Turkish aristocracy. The appointment gave Ibrahim power, riches and marriage to the sultan's sister, Princess Hatice. This was celebrated with great pomp and marked the summit of the ex-slave's standing. The alliance between Ibrahim and Roxelana gave rise to a palace faction. This included men like Alvise Gritti, the son of Andrea Gritti, Doge of Venice, born in Istanbul of a Turkish or Greek mother, and who, under the patronage of Ibrahim Pasha, had become Süleyman's counsellor for European affairs and treasurer for the kingdom of Hungary. The *devşirme* faction controlled the key points of the Empire, and by 1530 held considerable power. Ibrahim was Süleyman's *alter ego*, Gritti the supervisor of all European territories and an indispensable intermediary between the Christian world and that of the infidel. Roxelana was firmly ensconced in the sultan's heart.

Süleyman saw the explosive potential of this faction. Although vulnerable in his human relationships, he had a lucid political awareness. In 1534 Alvise Gritti was killed in Hungary, officially the victim of a revolution, but in fact deserted by the Ottoman government. Two years later, in 1536, Ibrahim Pasha was strangled on his return from an unsuccessful campaign against Iran and his property confiscated. Many complicated reasons contributed to the fall of these two powerful men. One was the death in 1534 of Hafsa, Süleyman's mother, who had been the grand vizier's influential patron and whose death had much weakened his position. Roxelana inherited the position of first lady and, in order to further her own faction, allied herself with Iskender Çelibi, Ibrahim's rival. Her manoeuvres with the sultan certainly contributed to the fall of the grand vizier.

Roxelana's principal concern now was to control the succession to the throne in favour of one of her sons. Through various initiatives she managed to create a strong and compact alliance, of which Mihrimah and her husband Rüstem Pasha were part. Rüstem had been a Serbian slave and was a diligent, sober and ambitious man, given to parsimony. Through the good graces of Mihrimah and Roxelana he gained the favour of Süleyman and swiftly advanced in his career, first as pasha, then as grand vizier. The 'little' red-faced Serb brought his own men with him to court, and soon they held many important government positions.

In the last decade of Süleyman's reign, the political struggle for succession to the throne was played out in Anatolia, then under attack by the Safavids. Rüstem Pasha frustrated the efforts of Prince Mustafa, Governor of Amasya, and supported Selim. Roxelana, with some justification, informed Süleyman of the prince's part in the plot. The result was the execution of Mustafa at Aktepe, near Konya on 5 October 1553. This was a political error on the part of Süleyman, who had allowed himself to be swayed by suspicion: by this act he removed the only prince who would have been able to govern the vast lands of the Crescent.

Süleyman was much criticized by the Janissaries and the Anatolian vassals for the execution of his son. Signs of a crisis began to appear, and in Rumelia in the west a serious revolt broke out, which was suppressed by Prince Beyazit in 1555. For Roxelana, Mustafa's death represented a personal and political triumph, at one stroke removing from the scene her ancient rival, Princess Gülbahar, and taking her own son Selim to the throne.

The figure of a royal princess dominates the city of Constantinople.
George De La Chappelle, *Recuel de divers portraits*, Paris, 1648. Venice, Biblioteca Nazionale Marciana.

THE SULTANATE OF THE WOMEN

New figures appeared on stage at the end of the sixteenth century. After the reign of Süleyman, the sultans distanced themselves more and more from the management of state affairs, and the running of the government passed into the hands of the women and palace slaves. Selim II (1566–74) mounted the throne and proved himself a man of few virtues, lustful, prone to excessive eating and drinking, to such an extent that he was known as *Sarhos*, 'The Sot'. The presence of Grand Vizier Sokullu Mehmet Pasha compensated for the fact that the new sultan had none of his father's gifts and ensured that the government was not immediately affected by the incompetence of the new sultan. It was Sokullu who, in fact, governed the state, proving himself a competent and firm statesman. Selim was succeeded by Murat III (1574–95), who was a reasonably competent administrator but whose passion for women led him astray.

The new dynamics that were now set up brought to the fore Cecilia Baffo-Venier, or Nur Banu, wife of Selim II and Murat's mother, a woman of indisputable political acumen. It was this *valide* who initiated what came to be known as the 'women's sultanate'. My Lady Light, as she was called at the palace, gave good political advice to her son and proved a loyal ally to Grand Vizier Sokullu. She approved of a government which managed to maintain balance and she was an excellent ambassadress, skilled in keeping the peace with enemies and renewing ties of friendship with Venice (1575), Iran (1574) and the Habsburgs (1577).

The first signs of the decline appeared when the grand vizier was assassinated in 1579. This was accompanied by growing dissenting movements and increasing corruption at all levels of the administrative and military system. A further step towards this

Portrait of Sultan Selim II, the son of Süleyman.
Codice Cicogna, *Memorie turchesche*, XVII century. Venice, Biblioteca del Museo Correr.

decline was the death of Nur Banu, who it was suspected had been poisoned. This sultana had governed the state with pragmatic and discreet competence and had shown herself to be a worthy heir of the Venetians from whom it is said she was descended.

The place of Nur Banu was taken by Safiye, 'The Pure One', in 1583. Events did not confirm the name of this beautiful sultana, beloved by Murat and mother of Mehmet III (1595–1603). Her tempestuous reign in the Sublime Porte began with a blood bath. Mehmet ordered nineteen brothers and twenty sisters to be killed, almost his only political act, since Safiye actually controlled all the affairs of state. There were eleven grand viziers in eighteen years; a great number of revolutions broke out in Anatolia due to a lack of continuity in policy and strong central government. Several significant defeats during the military campaigns undertaken at that time added to the disarray.

The seriousness of the situation was not that apparent, since the state appeared still to be powerful and in control of vast territories and much wealth. Delicate verses were being composed at court, the tenets of the Islamic faith were observed, tradition upheld. Ahmet I (1603–17) had the splendid Blue Mosque built in Istanbul, which outshone the splendours of its rival, the Byzantine basilica of Hagia Sopha. The relative peacefulness of Ahmet's reign was followed by a rapid succession of shadowy sultanates. For most of the time from 1617–51 the government was in the hands of Ahmed's wife, the sultana Kösem Mahpeyker, an ambitious and wilful woman. With her consent, Mustafa I, soon accused of madness, and Osman II, who was deposed and murdered in 1622, succeeded to the throne. The murder of Osman at the hands of his Janissaries had grave consequences, since this act destroyed the belief that the person of the sultan was sacrosanct and inviolable, one of the basic principles on which the state was founded.

Sultan Murat III had administrative experience but was distracted by his passion for women, and in politics he happily allowed himself to be guided by his mother, the fascinating Venetian Cecilia Baffo-Venier.
Codice Cicogna, *Memorie turchesche*, XVII century. Venice, Biblioteca del Museo Correr.

Kösem Mahpeyker governed with the support of the seraglio. She relied on the women of the harem and on the chief of the black eunuchs, and adopted a policy of political nepotism and a division of power, seen in the succession of grand viziers – eight between 1623 and 1632. Three were murdered and replaced with appointees deemed politically suitable at the moment. With the ascent to the throne of Murat IV (1623–40), it seemed that the power of the sultans might be restored. He was a young man, but determined to regain control of the situation. He reorganized the finances and administration and to a certain extent re-established the prestige of his government internationally. He was a champion of morality and religious virtues, and a person of considerable sensitivity and interested in intellectual pursuits.

Although deposed from power, Kösem was as yet unwilling to be set aside, and after Murat's brief reign she re-established her rule, placing Ibrahim on the throne. This sultan who suffered from bouts of insanity was totally incapable of governing, and thus the mechanism of rule by a puppet was re-introduced and with it the struggle between the factions at court, a succession of ministers, and the waste of huge resources. In 1648, by a second intervention by the Janissaries, Ibrahim was murdered and the palace was

THE MAD SULTAN: IBRAHIM I

Sultan Ibrahim I (1640–48), who passed into history as 'The Crazy One', cultivated only two passions: furs and women. During the unhappy years of his reign, Topkapí's pavilions were filled with precious furs, purchased at any price, or presented by ministers and functionaries wishing to advance their careers.

When not engaged in augmenting his fabulous collection, Ibrahim spent his time in the pleasures of the harem, a not surprising inclination that he shared with many of his ancestors, had he limited himself to the traditional presentation of expensive gifts. This sultan, like others, suffered from a serious mental illness and handed over to his favourites such state revenues as those paid by governors of his provinces.

While in the position of an absolute monarch whose wish was law, Ibrahim was, in fact, as much a slave as any other subject in the Ottoman Empire. The real power lay with two opposing factions. In the first years of Ibrahim's rule, government was in the hands of the wise Grand Vizier Kemankes, Kara Mustafa Pasha, who carried out internal reforms, and cultivated international friendships with other states. Once he had been eliminated in 1664, the control of public affairs passed to Cinci Hoca, the tutor of the sultan, and his mother, Kösem Mahpeyker.

The new government launched an offensive against Crete in order to restock the state finances, but their fight with Venice – which yielded no immediate results – ate heavily into the public purse. Conflict ensued and the Janissaries, who were paid poorly or not at all, rebelled and began to take more and more liberties. In the provinces the custodians of public property turned into feudal lords. Government positions, once handed out on merit and kept strictly under the control of the central government, were now sold to the highest bidder. To recoup the expense of the sumptuous gifts handed over to obtain their positions, the new government administrators sought to extract the maximum profit from their offices and preyed on their subordinates and on the population.

The degeneration of power encouraged corruption throughout the Empire, justice became uncertain, the system of 'clients', owed favours and money, became more and more extensive, and each official had to support a limitless number of dependants. The 'circle of parity', which had maintained a balance between different peoples and classes, between Muslim and infidel, the sultan and his subjects, and which, during the fifteenth and sixteenth centuries, had brought a huge number of Europeans to the Sublime Porte, began to break apart.

Ibrahim, quite indifferent to the chaotic situation, lived an existence based on pleasure alone, and due to the madness that was the curse of the House of Osman, was totally unaware of what was happening. Finally, on a stifling day in August 1648, the Janissaries massed menacingly in front of the Topkapí demanding the deposition of the grand vizier. The sultan refused, and the Janissaries decided to depose him. His mother, Kösem, sought in vain to save the life of her son. The time for agreements and negotiation had passed, and Ibrahim was strangled following an edict from the head of the Muslim wise men, in accordance with the laws of the Sublime Porte.

subjected to a struggle between Kösem's faction and that of the heir, Mehmet IV, supported by his mother Hatice Turhan. Eventually Kösem was ousted and she was strangled in 1651.

With the death of Kösem Mahpeyker a rather sombre period of Ottoman history drew to a close, although the Empire itself continued for centuries amid times alternating between light and darkness, decline and attempted reforms. When seeking the causes that provoked the crisis in the lands of the Crescent, many have been tempted to attribute these to the inordinate power of women and the harem. In fact, the decline was due to a series of missed opportunities. Unlike the Europeans, the Turks never managed to achieve the cultural and technological revolution of the sixteenth-century Renaissance. They did not take advantage of scientific progress and the Industrial Revolution, and instead took a series of unfortunate steps, while maintaining a retrograde and conservative outlook. The Sultanate of the Women was more a consequence than a cause. This era, and its political degeneration, highlights not only the *valides*, but a whole following of favourites, agents and eunuchs, who had a common cause in their feelings of inferiority and had lived a life of pain, loneliness and lack of affection. Through their immoderate use of power the women were trying to compensate for the grief they had endured and the high price they had paid to obtain the leading role on the ephemeral stage of the Ottoman court.

KÖSEM MAHPEYKER
A RECKLESS SULTANA

If a name can describe a destiny, that of Kösem Mahpeyker is a perfect example. Mahpeyker means 'Shape of the Moon', while Kösem is the word used to describe a bold and reckless person. The few portraits we have of this woman show her as slim and tall, with European features and a pale complexion, an evanescent figure with a powerful air of superiority and disdain which was particularly in evidence when she was portrayed among the delicate courtesans in her train.

It is thought that Kösem, born in 1589, was the daughter of a Greek Orthodox priest, and was first known as Anastasia. Sent as a gift from the Governor of Bosnia, she became the favourite of the young prince Ahmet I before he became sultan. Once firmly on the throne, first as the wife of Ahmet I and then as the mother of Mustafa I, Murat IV and Ibrahim I, and lastly as the grandmother of Mehmet IV, Kösem managed during forty-four years to raise the power of the *valide* sultan to the most powerful level it ever reached, thanks to a strategy of calculated manoeuvres.

Circumstances helped Kösem to realize her ambitions. Her plan was simple and efficacious. First she won over the women of the harem and the eunuchs, involving them in a web of favours from which they could extricate themselves only on pain of death. She was a careful negotiator with the opposition, and could skilfully use strategic retreats when circumstances required. In this manner Mahpeyker held on to power in the labyrinthine world of Ottoman politics for many years, and was only defeated after a long, bitter struggle instigated by the mother of Mehmet IV. The sad end to her life, in which she had made no concessions, was a violent death in August 1651.

Kösem showed surprising compassion for a woman used to buying subservience with wealth. Every year she would visit the prisons and she helped those charged with minor offences. She assisted the poor and provided a dowry for girls from poor families. She employed a large part of her patrimony usefully both in the capital and in the provinces of the Empire, subscribing to the canalization of the Nile at Cairo, providing rest houses for pilgrims at Mecca and Medina, and a caravanserai at Konya. The sultana was buried beside her husband, Ahmet I, in the gardens of the Blue Mosque.

The powerful ağa of the Janissaries and a page. *Foggie diverse del vestire de' Turchi*, XV century. Venice, Biblioteca Nazionale Marciana.

The grand vizier and other important
dignitaries. *Below*, some Janissary
functionaries.
Giulio Ferrario, *Il Costume antico e moderno*,
Milan, 1828. Venice, Biblioteca Nazionale
Marciana.

'THE WORLD IS THE PRISON HOUSE OF THE FAITHFUL
AND THE PARADISE OF THE INFIDEL'

Mehmet IV was six years old when he came to the throne of the Sublime Porte in 1648. It was, therefore, the wise Hatice Turhan, the mother of the young man, who dominated the political scene in the second half of the seventeenth century, together with the powerful Köprülü family. She had been born in the Ukraine and had been kidnapped by the Tartars. A tall and elegant woman with blue eyes, she was swift to act but well balanced in her judgements and, as regent, she took an active part in politics. The office of grand vizier was in the hands of the Köprülü family, who came originally from Albania. Mehmet Köprülü and his son Fazíl Ahmet brought back stable government by their firm and forceful policy, which had as its objective the improvement of finances, the re-establishment of order and of Ottoman prestige abroad.

They set about ridding the government of the excesses that had caused so much damage and curbed the power of the *valide* sultan and the harem. Hatice Turhan took an active part in these reforms, of which she thoroughly approved, and gave her support by gradually withdrawing from the affairs of state. Like other royal princesses, she instigated and financed charitable projects. Although the intellectual and artistic output at the time was on the wane, attempts were still being made to produce new public buildings. Hatice Turhan built the Yeni Camí, or New Mosque, at Eminönü; although it was not very innovative, it was elegant and firmly linked to the style of the imperial mosques, of which it is the last example.

The construction of caravanserai and markets, however, testifies to the lively trade that flourished. In 1660 the Egyptian bazaar was opened, exclusively for the sale of spices, drugs, plants and medicinal herbs. The Enlightenment in Turkey introduced a new mentality which welcomed not only reform and change, but also a new approach to Western learning, technology and customs. The whole Turkish Empire was full of European artists, painters, scientists, diplomats and observers, who wanted to learn about the still-mysterious world of the Ottomans. For the first time, the Turks began to respond, instead of maintaining the attitude of disdainful superiority that they had cultivated. Finally they allowed themselves to feel some curiosity about the West.

Had this desire for renewal been shared by all those in power, the Ottoman Empire might have made a sudden leap forward and become a modern state. As it was, conservative elements proved tenaciously strong, and there was a harsh battle between reformers and reactionaries throughout the eighteenth century. The palace was, on the whole, on the side of the reformers, and Ahmet III (1702–30), a cultured, melancholic man who loved flowers and birds and women, shared the new interest in Western culture.

The Ottoman court, elegant and frivolous, gave itself over to the cultivation of flowers, particularly tulips, which were grown in the secret imperial gardens where wonderful new varieties were bred. So intense was this passion that this period

following pages
The eighteenth century introduced new ideas into Turkey. There was a desire for reform and change as a result of Western knowledge, technology and customs.
Jean-Baptiste Huysmans, *In the Harem*.
London, Mathaf Gallery.

became known as the Tulip Era. At this time was born the idea of an Ottoman embassy to France, a strange and powerful conception which came into effect when Mehmet Efendi Yirmisekiz travelled there in 1720–21.

The effect of the discoveries made by an Ottoman nobleman, tied to tradition but intellectually curious, brought changes even to the most famous of all harems. The women of the Tulip Era, already in love with flowers, modernity and all things new, allowed themselves to be carried away by the seductive breeze of renewal that came from Europe. The trend spread throughout Istanbul and became known as the 'French fashion', a kind of reversal of Western taste for things Turkish. Mehmet Efendi Yirmisekiz brought back from Europe a vision of a new world, one vastly different from the Ottoman Empire, with no grand viziers and no harems, and which became tangible through the hundreds of prints of castles, villas and French gardens which were already in fashion in Istanbul. His was a vision which materialized through theatrical spectacles and microscopes; through such inebriating pleasures as the thousand bottles of Champagne and the nine hundred Burgundy wines that the diplomat brought back with him. It is understandable that in this whirlwind of sensations the ambassador should exclaim as he stood in the gardens of the château at Marly: 'The world is the prison house of the Faithful, and the Paradise of the Infidel'.

The sultan and his women imitated the fashion of the French court, and had the little summer palace of Kagithane on the outskirts of Istanbul turned into a version of Versailles or Fontainebleau. The swiftness with which it was transformed into a French residence was incredible, and here the ladies of the seraglio came to enjoy quite new sensations. The important *valide* of that era – Mehpâre Emetüllah Râbia Gülnûs (*c.*1647–1715), the mother of Ahmet III; Sâliha Sebkatí (*c.*1680–1739), the mother of Mahmut I; Sehsüvâr (*c.*1682–1756), the mother of Osman III; Mihrisah (1745–1805), the mother of Selim III; and the imperial princesses – all commissioned European architects to erect their fountains and buildings in a rococo style which mixed oriental features with European decorative motifs.

The ladies of the upper classes began, hesitantly, to open the doors of their harems to European ladies living in Istanbul. Until that time a mutual diffidence had kept them apart. The older and more conservative Turkish ladies had refused to meet the European women, who lived mainly in the European quarters of Galata and Pera. For they were for the most part the wives of ambassadors and rich merchants, and had shown little interest in Ottoman culture and habits. When a gap appeared in this wall

The desire for reform was also apparent at court and Sultan Ahmet III, a cultured and melancholic man, gave his permission for a court dignitary to pay an official visit to France for the first time.
Istanbul, Topkapí, Resim Galerisi.

of diffidence, mutual problems and feelings were discovered by both groups, and the distance that separated the two worlds no longer seemed so overwhelming. Lady Mary Wortley Montagu stayed in Istanbul during the reign of Ahmet III. Reluctant to waste her time with the conventional frivolities of social life in Pera, she was one of the first European women to establish contact with the women of the Ottoman world. Her descriptions offer a realistic and truthful impression of their lives and place Turkish women in a new light. There had been many male accounts of the harem, invariably second-hand and more often than not coloured for the benefit of Western readers. Lady Montagu revealed the most unsuspected behaviour, such as the spontaneity of the women in the harem in contrast to their formal and composed behaviour in public, where all sentiments, even of happiness had to be moderated. In the harem Turkish women gave free reign to their dreams, passions and thoughts, disproving the usual harsh criticism of Muslim society. They had a certain economic freedom, thanks to a dowry commensurate with the wealth of their husbands, which they could call upon in the event of a separation. They were not recluses because family ties were very strong, and were not caught up in the toils of religious interdicts which forbade autopsy and scientific experiments. Although ignorant, they were capable of thinking, and were in charge of childbearing and childbirth. They made use of vaccination and practised preventive cures against smallpox which were still unknown in Europe.

Ottoman women were not just concerned with how to remain beautiful; some were writers, and in the eighteenth century poets like Zübeyde Fitnan Haním left their mark on literature. Even in the ultra-formal Imperial Harem relationships between men and women were evolving: the favourites no longer had to snake their way up the beds of their lord, nor were they chosen for his pleasure by tossing an embroidered handkerchief in their direction. There were certainly problems and contradictions in the lives of Eastern women, but seen from within, the harem was a living organism, where life bubbled, full of ideas and vitality.

Sultan Mehmet IV, who came to power in 1648 at the age of six and who was on the throne of the Ottoman Empire until 1687.
Istanbul, Topkapí, Resim Galerisi.

facing page
The splendid decoration of Sultan Ahmet III's dining room.
Istanbul, Topkapí.

The young sultana Nakşidil, the mother of Mehmet II (1808–39), is said to have belonged to a noble family from Martinique. Her name was Aimée Dubuc de Rivery, and she was the cousin of the Empress Josephine, the first wife of Napoleon Bonaparte. Nakşidil was kidnapped during a sea voyage and sold to the Bey of Algiers, who presented her to Sultan Abdül Hamit I (1774–89). Beautiful, with large blue eyes, she was reserved, intelligent and well brought up and soon captured the sultan's heart. Aimée de Rivery has been regarded by some not only as the instigator of westernization at the Ottoman court but as the inspiration of Mehmet II's modernist politics.

THE EMPRESS MIHRIŞAH IN THE ERA OF ENLIGHTENMENT

The wave of reform which swept the Turkish Empire in the eighteenth century brought many changes to the imperial court. It modified the relationship between the sultan and his ladies and transformed the role of the sultana mother. The Princess Mihrişah, mother of Sultan Selim III (1789–1807), was a willing protagonist of the reforms.
She was born about 1745, it is not known precisely where, and as a young girl entered the harem of Mustafa III, soon becoming his favourite. Selim, the future sultan, was born in 1761 from their union. Mihrişah was a genuinely religious woman and followed the most fundamental principles of Islam. This reserved and peace-loving woman developed in her son an open mind and a love for the arts and sciences as well as an interest in exploring the spiritual and mystical aspects of the world about him. Brought up in this liberal climate, Selim III became a man of the Enlightenment and a precursor of the nineteenth-century reformers, propelling the Empire towards a new phase in its development. His changes included bringing the army up to date by setting up a military school and creating a new body of infantry trained by European officers.
Mihrişah shared in her son's reforms especially the modernizing of the military schools and the establishing of a diplomatic corps. During Selim's reign a truly revolutionary change took place in this field: the Muslim law prohibiting the Faithful from living in the land of the infidel was revoked, and permanent ambassadors could be sent to such major European capitals as London, Vienna and Paris. The experiment enjoyed only limited success, since the appointees had not received adequate training and had no knowledge of foreign languages. However, this created the nucleus of the future Ottoman diplomatic corps.
The sultana Mihrişah took little part in politics, and the rare occasions she approached the sultan were in order to beg a favour or an act of mercy. Her piety led her towards mysticism, and both she and her son were members of the Mevlana sect of Sufi mystics, the so-called Dancing Dervishes. Choosing a contemplative life, Mihrişah chose to live in the Eyüp quarter, on a hill overlooking the Golden Horn, a lush green place, filled with silence and peace, and considered by the Muslims to be the holiest site in Istanbul due to the presence of the mausoleum of Eyüp Ensari, the standard-bearer of Mohammed.
From this spiritual place, Mihrişah directed an extensive programme for the creation of religious foundations, and she had a vast library containing precious illuminated manuscripts and rare books. She died on 16 October 1805 and did not witness the sad fall of her son, who was forced to abdicate in the reactionary revolt of the Janissaries.

The dates may not coincide and the origins of French influence at the Turkish court may be more complex, nevertheless, the reign of the sultana from Martinique shows how, even as late as the nineteenth century, the harem was still seen as a place of mystery and intrigues skilfully sustained by princesses and eunuchs. Writers of the Romantic period in Europe nourished the myth of the Orient, fearful that it would be strangled by the realities of industrialization. That 'egalitarian wind poisoned by smoke' then blowing in Europe, drove them towards the East, where mystery, charm and unbridled luxury could still be found.

While Romantic writers were idealizing the aesthetic and hedonistic virtues of Turkish life, the Turks were suddenly filled with doubts about their past and uncertain of their future. Throughout the nineteenth century, there was a clash between the forces of innovation and tradition as several interested parties joined in the struggle. The sultans and the *valide*, hiding behind their opulent, complex and seemingly immutable protocol, began to watch with growing interest the way things were developing in Europe. Sultan Abdül Mecit I (1839–61) spoke

Myths about the Levant were encouraged in Europe by those Romantic writers who feared the egalitarian winds of industrialization and sought a more exotic life in the East.
Venice, Caffè Florian.

Modern ideas became contagious and
the doors of the harem were opened
to European women living in Istanbul.
The ladies of the upper classes were
the first to adopt French fashions, but
traditional costume was still worn by
the people.
Turchia Album di 62 foto, n.d. Venice,
Biblioteca Nazionale Marciana.

The magnificent palace of Princess
Hatice, the sister of Selim III, at
Defterdar Burnu.
Ignaz Mellin, *Voyage pittoresque de
Constantinople et du Bosphore*, Paris, 1819.
Parma Biblioteca Pal;atina

facing page
The sultana mother's reception room, cluttered with Western-style furniture although the architecture was traditional, could be a metaphor for the contrast between the old and the new which was tearing apart the Ottoman Empire.
Istanbul, Dolmabahçe Palace.

Imperial bath in alabaster. In the nineteenth century the court and the sultans left the Topkapí for the Dolmabahçe Palace on the banks of the Bosporus, an eclectic and majestic residence.
Istanbul, Dolmabahçe Palace.

> 'The women keep the ancient veil and the overgarment which hides their shape, but the veil has become transparent and allows one to glimpse a little hat with a feather, and the garment often covers a dress modelled in Paris.'
> *Turchia Album di 62 foto*, n.d. Venice, Biblioteca Nazionale Marciana.

RAHIME PERESTÜ
THE LAST OTTOMAN QUEEN

The intelligent and fascinating Rahime Perestü, the fourth wife of Abdül Mecit I (1839–61), was very small, with a heart-shaped face, large blue eyes and blonde hair. Known as Perestü, 'The Little Swallow', she attracted the favour of the sultan purely on the merit of her beauty and charm, for she was sterile and no son could ever cement her union with the Lord of the Turks. Many things, however, had changed over the course of the centuries. In the past no woman could ever have dreamed of reaching the summit of Empire without bearing sons, but at the height of the Romantic period in the mid-nineteenth century, the Ottoman court put aside the demand to be woman and mother.

One of Abdül Mecit's wives, a very young Circassian slave, had died of consumption, leaving the little Abdül Hamit an orphan. The sultan decided to give the child an adoptive mother and chose Perestü, both as a consolation for her sterility and to show his appreciation of her many qualities. Abdül Hamit at first rejected Perestü's love. He was morbidly attached to the memory of his own mother and had become solitary and introverted. Only with time did the young prince come to accept and repay the understanding, tolerance and affection that Perestü gave him.

The last *valide* sultan, Perestü was born in about 1830 and we know little of her origins and early life. She was well balanced, understood the workings of the human heart, and was able to steer through the unhappy years of Abdül Hamit's reign by keeping her distance from the political scene. In no way did she contribute to the emancipation of Turkish women but managed instead to keep the affection of her diffident and reactionary stepson, since she represented his idea of Turkish womanhood.

Contrary to her nickname, Perestü did not swoop through life with the thoughtless gaiety of a swallow, but ruled the harem with the severity of a mother superior. Abdül Hamit's harem was sober and discreet, and had the minimum number of women required by etiquette. The girls were not there for nights of unbridled love or to satisfy the lustful passion of the sultan, since, as one of his women put it: 'this man was one of the most courteous and understanding of masters, but he never loved anyone, including himself'. As the century drew to a close, the qualities that were most appreciated and demanded at the Ottoman court were politeness, courtesy, composure and good manners.

An historical account of the meeting between Perestü and the Empress Augusta, wife of the German Kaiser Wilhelm, during a state visit that took place in the reign of Abdül Hamit are most interesting. During this early morning encounter, the *valide* sultan in her dazzling Asiatic costume appeared anachronistic and almost pathetic as she stood in the magnificent rooms of the harem, filled with kitsch Viennese armchairs, dozens of cuckoo clocks and priceless Chinese porcelain.

The last sultana died in 1904 in Macka Palace, which had just been granted to her by her brother-in-law, Abdül Aziz, and was buried, like many of the Osman royalty, in the cemetery of Eyüp, a burial ground much admired by European Romantics.

274. Dame turque.   P. Sebah

French and appreciated the arts and sciences. He and his mother, Bezmialem (c.1807–53), a sensitive and vivacious woman, were regarded as innovators.

At the beginning of the century the lords of the Crescent left the Topkapí and moved to the Dolmabahçe Palace on the shores of the Bosporus designed by a young Armenian architect. This majestic and eclectic mansion, whose white marbled walls were tinted with blue reflections of sky and sea, became the seat of the new court. New blood was introduced in the form of jurists, technocrats and men of letters. They set about building a modern world, made plans for recodifying antiquated laws, for secularizing education and introducing new forms of government. All these plans were praiseworthy but, of course, once put into action appeared as a contradiction of Ottoman realities, much as the appartments in the new harem, laid out in the traditional way but filled with Western furniture and decoration, appeared totally out of place.

Life for the sultan's women slowly but steadily began to change during the nineteenth century. Transformations took place which opened a breach in the wall that had isolated them. The princesses now received a broader education than in the past, and gradually, under the supervision of the eunuchs, began to venture out of the palace and contact the outside world.

Pertevniyel, the mother of the progressive Sultan Abdül Aziz (1861–76), was *valide* at this time (c.1812–83). Her son was so fascinated with European taste that he actually ventured into the world of the infidel. It was only a short journey, but one of immense importance, since it was unprecedented in Ottoman history.

The charitable and religious Pertevniyel occupied herself with pious works and did not interfere in the politics of her son. She is forever linked to the mosque in the Aksaray quarter. Her place was taken for only a few months by the Princess Sevkefza (1820–89), the mother of the liberal Murat V. A mason, who liked to surround himself with businessmen and liberal authors, Murat suffered from bouts of madness. Upon his death on 29 August 1904, in the sinister palace of Çirağan on the shores of the Bosporus, not far from Dolmabahçe, the women of his harem were given permission to marry.

In the summer of 1876, when Murat V abdicated in favour of his brother Abdül Hamit II (1876–1909), the population acclaimed the newly elected sultan as a liberal and innovator. He was ugly, and had a pale complexion and aquiline nose. Diffident and nervous, he soon belied the expectations of his supporters and proved as authoritarian a sovereign as his nickname, 'The Red Sultan', suggests. Abdül Hamit was a despot who managed to lay his hands on vast power by continually changing grand viziers. He promoted both pan-Islamism and nationalism, causing considerable tension among the peoples who made up the Empire. He re-established his pastoral role as caliph-sultan, abolished the constitution and dissolved parliament which had only been in place for a year. During the reign of this sultan, for the first time in Ottoman history, the *valide* was an adoptive mother. When he was orphaned at the age of six, Rahime Perestü had been entrusted with the young prince by Abdül Mecit. She was also the last empress, since the mothers of the last two descendants of the Osmanli line were dead when their sons mounted the throne

Under The Red Sultan the emancipation of women was reined back. Women of the upper classes had already adopted Western customs, thanks to the influence of the

Ottoman women loved to be in the open air. Accompanied by servants and eunuchs they often took trips to the outskirts of Constantinople.
Istanbul, Topkapí, Resim Galerisi.

press and their European counterparts. Ottoman women had had a taste of freedom. The streets of Istanbul teemed with their comings and goings. They still wore the veil, but now it was transparent, so as to reveal their features, and under their brilliantly coloured ankle-length garments, they wore daring French dresses. Abdül Hamit tried to impose a more rigorous comportment, and in 1901 issued an edict forbidding women to frequent the shops of European merchants. They were told to use a veil of a specific thickness and length, and were obliged to have an escort when out on the street, under pain of arrest.

Mehmet IV, the last ruler of the Ottomans, reigned from 1918 to 1922. Istanbul, Topkapí, Resim Galerisi.

In this aggressive climate the Imperial Harem suffered the strictest observation of regulations, and the ladies were forced to live in seclusion in the splendid isolation of the Dolmabahçe. Gossip had it that, in defiance of all his own rules, the sultan himself was under the sway of the independent and fascinating Belgian, Flora Cordier, a liberated woman and the proprietor of her own shop. However, progress towards modernization had not been in vain, and the process of emancipation could not be halted by a backward sultan. Women took an active part in the revolt of the Young Turks which broke out in July 1908, campaigned for the veil to be abolished and for the right to participate in public events. In those years women's groups were formed, some with philanthropic aims, others more radical. Although these were limited to upper-class women, they were a link with the European feminist movement and promoted a women's press and writings.

Upon the deposition of The Red Sultan in 1909, the mysterious world of the harem underwent a traumatic upheaval. When the old seraglio was turned into offices for the Ministry of Defence, the women of the deceased sultans had been transferred to the Topkapí, which in turn had been abandoned by the court in favour of the new harem. The government of the Young Turks debated the suppression of the harem and, with a surprizingly modern outlook, advertised in the newspapers for relatives and families to fetch the sultan's favourites who were still living in total segregation. The seraglio, which had always been the most secret and intimate place of the Lords of the Altai suddenly ceased to exist, and the last scene to be played out was a procession of intimidated and disoriented women leaving the palace.

The last two descendants of the house of Osman were Mehmet V (1909–18) and Mehmet VI (1918–22), but despite their glorious names they retained only the shadow of power. During the First World War and in the disastrous post-war years, the sultans faded into mere illusion. New legislation overturned the laws governing marriage and divorce and laid the foundations of equal partnership between men and women. While the whole country was in turmoil, a much-reduced harem lived out its time in the palace of Dolmabahçe.

In the now useless but still magnificent halls of the Imperial Palace, the elegant, ethereal princesses wandered about like ghosts, dressed in the best of French fashions. They and their sultan knew only too well that it was time to retire and clear the stage for a new leader who would transform the Empire into a republic and, in 1926, would abolish polygamy and formally establish equality between men and women.

Ethereal, refined and flirtatious, dressed in the height of French fashion, the last of the Ottoman sultanas wander like phantoms in the uselessly splendid halls, knowing that the time has come for them to give way to a new leader.
Turchia Album di 62 foto, n.d. Venice, Biblioteca Nazionale Marciana.

BIBLIOGRAPHY

ALDERSON A.D., *The Structure of the Ottoman Dynasty*, Oxford, 1956.
AMICIS (DE) E., *Costantinopoli*, vol. 2, Milan, 1877.
ANGIOLELLO G.M., *Historia Turchesca*, 1480.
ARBEL B., "Nur Banu (c. 1530-83): a Venetian Sultana?", in *Turcica*, 24 (1992), pp. 241-59.
Art décoratif ottoman (L'), published under the direction of Yanni Petsopoulos, Paris 1982.

BASSANO L., *Costumi et i modi particolari della vita de' Turchi*, Rome, 1545.
BAUDIER M., *Histoire Général du Serrail et de la cour du Grand-Seigneur Empereur des Turcs*, Lyons, 1659.
BELGIOIOSO TRIVULZIO C., *Scenes de la vie turque*, Paris, 1858.
BERCHET J.C., *Le voyage en Orient*, 1992.
BON O., *Descrizione del Serraglio del Gransignore*, Venice, 1865.

CARRETTO G.E., *Gem Sultan Pellegrino d'Oriente*, Paese, 1991.
CARRETTO G.E., *I Turchi del Mediterraneo*, Rome, 1989.
CARRETTO G.E., *Un sultano prigioniero del Papa*, Venice, 1989.
CELARIE H., *Les derniers harems*, Paris, 1993.
CERASI M., *La città' del Levante*, Milan, 1986.
CHIERICI A., *Vera Relatione della Città di Costantinopoli, et in particolare del Serraglio del Gran Turco*, Bracciano, 1621.
CLOT A., *Solimano il Magnifico*, Milan, 1986.
COCO C., *La lussuria del viver turchesco*, Venice, 1990.
COCO C., POLACCO R. and RINALDI S., *Bisanzio, Costantinopoli, Istanbul. Storia e arte di una città imperiale*, Venice, 1994.
CROUTIER LYTLE A., *Harem. The World Behind the Veil*, New York, 1989.

DASIPPE G., *Storia Secreta della famiglia ottomana*, Naples, 1729.

EBERSOLT J., *Constantinople et les voyageurs français du Levant*, Paris, 1919.

FERRARIO G., *Il Costume antico e moderno di tutti i popoli*, vol. IV, Milan, 1823.

GAUTIER TH., *Constantinople*, Paris, 1991.
GOODWIN G., *A History of the Ottoman Empire*, London, 1971.

HAMMER (VON) J., *Histoire de l'Empire ottoman*, vol. 18, Paris, 1835-43.
HARRY M., *Les derniers harems*, Paris, 1933.
HASLIP J., *Il Sultano*, Milan, 1992.
Histoire de l'Empire Ottoman, edited by R. Mantran, Paris, 1992.

KOMAN M., *Eyüp Sultan Loti Kahvesi ve Çevresi*, Istanbul, 1986.

LOTI P., *Aziyadé*, Paris, 1991.

MANDEL G., *Storia dell'harem*, Milan, 1992.
MANTRAN R., *Istanbul dans la seconde moitie du XVII siecle*, Paris, 1962.
MANTRAN R., *La vita quotidiana a Costantinopoli ai tempi di Solimano il Magnifico*, Milan, 1985.
MEHMED EFENDI, *Les paradis des infideles*, Paris, 1981.
MENAVINO G.A., *I Costumi e la vita de Turchi*, Florence, 1551.
MILLER B., *Beyond the Sublime Porte: The Grand Seraglio of Stambul*, New Haven, 1941.
MONTAGU M., *L'Islam au péril des femmes*, Paris, 1983.
MUSSI N., *Relatione sulla città di Costantinopoli e Serraglio, con i riti de i Turchi...*, Bologna and Bassano, 1675.

NERVAL (DE) G., *Voyage en Orient*, vol. 2, Paris, 1884.

OSMAN BEY, *Les femmes de Turquie*, Paris, 1878.

PENZER N.M., *The Harem*, Philadelphia and London, 1936.
PETIS DE LA CROIX F., *Etat général de l'Empire ottoman*, Paris, 1695.
POUQUEVILLE F.C.H., *Viaggio in Morea, a Costantinopoli ed in Albania...*, vol. 2, Milan, 1816.

RAMBERTI B., *Delle cose de Turchi*, vol. 3, Vinegia, 1541.
REFIK A., *Kadïnlar Saltanatï*, Istanbul, 1924.

REFIK A., *Kïzlar Agasï*, Istanbul, 1926.

REFIK A., *Turhan Valide*, Istanbul, 1931.

Relazioni degli ambasciatori veneti al Senato, edited by E. Alberi, series III, vol. 3, Florence, 1840-55.

ROSSI E., "La sultana Nur Banu (Cecilia Venier-Baffo) moglie di Selim II (1566-1574) e madre di Murad III (1574-1595)", in *Oriente Moderno*, 11 (1953), pp. 433-41.

ROUX J.P., *La Turquie*, Paris, 1953.

ROUX J.P., *Storia dei Turchi*, Milan, 1988.

RYCAUT P., *Istoria dello Stato presente dell'Imperio Ottomano*, Venice, 1672.

SALMON T., Lo *Stato presente di tutti i popoli del mondo*, vol. VI, Venice, 1738.

SANUDO M., *I Diarii*, vol. 53, Venice, 1879-1903.

SHAW S., *History of the Ottoman Empire and Modern Turkey*, vol. 2, Cambridge, 1976-77.

SPAGNI E., "Una Sultana Veneziana", in *Nuovo Archivio Veneto*, XIX (1900), pp. 241-348.

SPANDUGINO Th., *I Commentari...*, Fiorenza, 1551.

TAVERNIER G.B., *Relatione del Serraglio Interiore, et Esteriore del Gran Signore*, Rome, 1682.

THEVENOT J., *Voyages au Levant et en Asie*, Paris, 1664.

TUGLACI P., *Osmanlï döneminde Istanbul kadïnlarï,* Istanbul, 1984.

TUGLACI P., *Osmanlï Saray kadïnlarï,* Istanbul, 1985.

VAMBERY A., "Personal Recollections of Abdul Hamid and His Court", in *Nineteenth Century*, 1909.

GLOSSARY

acemi oğlan	Young pages of Christian origin who were forcibly recruited from the provinces of the Empire to perform the most menial tasks
Akhor Kapí	Stable Gate
Altïnyol	A long corridor, the Golden Way, decorated with fine ceramics
Araba Kapísí	Carriage Gate
Arz Odasí	Throne Room
Bab-í Hümayün	Imperial Gate
Bab-í-Saadet	Gate of Felicity, Door of the White Eunuchs
Bab-üs Selam	Gate of Salutations
Baghdad Köskü	Pavilion of Baghdad
Balík Hane Kapísí	Fish Gate
baltacï	The sultan's halberdiers
baskâtibe	First secretary responsible for discipline and order in the harem
baş kadín	Mother of the first born and heir presumptive to the throne, first lady
baş musahib	Chamberlain, liaison between the sultan and the sultana's staff
berber usta	Woman in charge of shaving the sultan who directed the girl barbers
bey	Gentleman
birun	The public, external area of the seraglio housing government offices
börek	Very thin layers of pastry filled with cheese and then fried
bostancí	The sultan's gardeners
çamaşïrlik	Laundry of the harem
çamaşïr usta	Overseer of the laundry
camekân	Large hall used for undressing in the baths
cariye	Girls, slaves, novices
Cariyeler Dairesi	Apartments of the sultan's slaves or novices
Cariyeler Hamamí	Slaves' baths
Cariyeler Hastanesí	Hospital of the harem
Cariyeler Mutfaklar	Small kitchen for the slaves
çavuş	Sultan's guards
Çesmeli Sofa	Vestibule of the Fountain
cevze	Small pot for making Turkish coffee
cirid	Tournament in which young men on Arab horses jousted with wooden javelins
çubuk	Long pipe
Deftarhane	Chancellery
Degirmen Kapí	Mill Gate
Demir Kapí	Iron Gate, leading to the gardens
devetlu	'She who has power'; title of respect given to the sultan's mother
devşirme	Forced recruitment of Christian subjects within the Ottoman Empire
Divan	Government
dizlik	Long underwear
Dolaplí Kubbe	A dark antechamber guarded day and night by two black eunuchs
dolma	stuffed vegetables
enderun	The internal area of the seraglio, the residence of the court, the harem and the sultan
entari	A waistcoat with a narrow waist worn open or buttoned
Eski Saray	The old palace
ferace	Long shapeless overgarment reaching the ankle
gazel	Traditional lyric poems
gedikli	Young girls upon whom the lord had 'rested his gaze'
halvet	'Retreat'. A warning call that the Sultan wished to walk about with his ladies
hamam	Public baths
Hamam Yolu	A corridor
hançer	Small sharp dagger
haním sultan	Literally 'Lady sultana'
Haramgah	Archaic term for harem
Harem Çamaşïrlïk	Huge room used as as the laundry
Harem-i-Hümayun	Imperial Harem

Harema ağalar Dairesi	Apartments of the black eunuchs
haremlík	Area reserved exclusively for the women
harim	Archaic term for harem
haseki sultan	Used since the sixteenth century for the wives of the great lord
Hastalar Kapísí	Gate of the Sick
hastalar usta	Chief nurse
hatun	In early Ottoman times the wives of the great lord
havuz	Pool
Hazine	Inner Treasury
hazinedar ağa	Treasurer of the harem
Hazinedar Dairesi	Apartment of the harem's chief treasurer
hazinedar usta	Chief treasurer of the harem
Hekimbaşí Odasí	The apartment of the chief physician which is in a tower and looks like a prison
hennè	Powder used to dye the hair, nails, hands and feet
Hirkai Şerif Odasí	A special pavilion containing the 'most holy things', sacred relics of Islam
hoca	Tutor
hosaf	A drink made from steeped raisins, rosewater and mead
Hünkâr Hamamí	Royal baths
Hünkâr Sofasí	Hall of the Emperor
hünkâr sofasí	Hall equipped for spectacles
ibriktar usta	Superindendant of the baths
iç oğlan	Boys of the internal household
iftar	Break in the *Ramadan* fast
Iftariye	Small bronze canopy facing the sea
ikbal	The sultan's favourites
ippetlu	Literally 'She who has dignity', a title of respect for the sultan's mother
jinn	Evil spirits and imps who inhabit stagnant water
kadí	Islamic judge
kadín	A favourite who gives birth to a son
kadín or kadín efendi	Terms which correspond to the title of lady
Kafes	Literally 'cage'
kahveci usta	Coffee steward
kalfa	Older servants
kalpak	Winter headgear of fur or heavy velvet and perhaps embroidered with pearls
kanun	Zither
kapí ağasí	Head of the white eunuchs or grand master
kapící	Guards, doormen
karagöz	Turkish shadow theatre
kazan	Cauldron
kebab	Traditional meat dishes
kethüda	Supervisor in charge of the staff and the running of various departments
kil	Clay used for cleaning the hair
Kiler Koğuşu	Dispensary
kilerci usta	Person in charge of the dispensary
kízlar ağasí	Head of the black eunuchs and the sultana's foreign minister
Kízlarağasï Dairesí	Apartment of the chief of the black eunuchs
köçek oyunu	Traditional dance performed by men dressed as women
Kubbealtí	Council Chamber
Kurban Bayramí	Feast of the Sacrifice, during which the head of every family must ritually slaughter and sacrifice a ram
Kuşhane Kapísí	Gate of the Aviary leading into the Third Court
kutucu usta	Personal maid
mâbeyin	Sultan's private apartment
medrese	religious school
Meyyit Kapísí	Gate of the Dead
Musahiban Dairesi	Mistress of ceremonies
musahip kadín	Educated and cultured woman of the sultan's private entourage
nahil	Wax decorations of trees, animals and flowers created by specialized craftsmen often with silver thread and precious stones
namaz	Prayer
Nevruz	First day of the year and the beginning of spring
nilüfer	Sorbet made from the distilled liquid of a plant shaped like a horseshoe
Nöbetyeri	Black eunuchs' guard room
Ocaklí Sofa	Room with a Hearth

oda	Servants who performed the complex routines of court life
Odun Kapísí	Fuel Gate
Onluk Kapí	Gate of the Ten
Orta Kapí	Median Gate
Osman III Köşkü	Osman III's kiosk
pekmez	Drink made from the must of raisins
rakí or arak	Drink flavoured with aniseed, also known as 'Lion's Milk'
Ramadan	Month of fasting
Rivan Köşk ül	The Pavilion of Erivan, Room of the Turban
santur	Psaltery
saray	Palace
Saray Burnu	Cape of the Seraglio
saray usta	Mistress of ceremonies in the harem
Sarík Odasí	Room of the Turban
saz	musical instrument
selamlík	Area of the home reserved for men
serbet	Sorbet
sïcaklïk	Room in the baths corresponding to the *calidarium*
Sofa	Small waiting room
Sofa Köşkü	Kiosk of Mustafa Pasha
Soğuk Çeşme Kapísí	Gate of the Fountain
spadoni	Eunuchs whose testicles had been cut off
Sultan Ibrahim Kameriyesi	Marble terrace
Sünnet Odasí	Chamber of the Circumcision, reserved exclusively for the rites of the royal princes
sütnine	Wet-nurses
şalvar	Wide trousers narrowing at the ankle
şehadet	Religious formula:'Allah is great and Mohammed is his Prophet'
Şeker Bayramï	Sugar Festival marking the end of fasting
tabla	Trays set on low stools used as tables
tavşan oyunu	A popular dance
tellâk	Servants assigned to the baths
thlibiae	Eunuchs whose testicles had been crushed
tomak	Game in which teams competed with a ball on a rope
Topkapí	Cannon Gate
turşu	Pickled greens
usta	Women in charge of the servants and slaves
vakíf	Inspector of charitable foundations
valide alay	Cortège which accompaies the mother of the new sultan to the Imperial Residence
valide sultan	Mother of the sultan
vekil usta	Woman prefect of the slaves
yaşmak	Veil covering hair and face, leaving only eyes exposed
Yemek Odasí	Dining Room
Yeni Kütüphane	New Library
Yeni Saray	New Palace
zanana	Archaic term for harem

PHOTOGRAPHIC ACKNOWLEDGEMENTS

Bassano, Pinacoteca 12, 140-141

Besançon, Musée des Beaux-Arts et Archéologie, photography by Ch. Choffet 64-65

Bologna, Biblioteca dell'Archiginnasio, photography by Magic Vision 48, 54, 58, 66, 67, 69, 72, 73, 74, 80, 82, 91, 93, 98, 120, 131, 144-145

Bourg-en-Bresse, Collection Musée de Brou, museum photographs 78-79

Istanbul, T.C. Kültür Bakanligi, Topkapí Sarayi Müzesi Müdürlügü 53, 75, 116, 119, 156, 159, 166, 172, 173, 184

Liverpool, Board of Trustees of the National Museums and Galleries on Merseyside (Walker Art Gallery) 142-143

London, Courtesy Chaucer Fine Arts Ltd 8-9

London, Courtesy Mathaf Gallery 16-17, 126-127, 133, 136-137, 152-153, 160-161, 170-171

London, reproduced with the permission of the Trustees of the Wallace Collection 22-23

London, Sotheby's Picture Library 157

London, Venturi Francesco 42-43, 45, 46, 47, 56, 57, 83, 84, 88, 89, 92, 97, 100, 101, 106-107, 123, 130, 140, 175, 180, 181

Nantes, A.G., Ville de Nantes, Musée des Beaux-Arts 102-103, 109

Naples, Luciano Pedicini, Archivio dell'Arte 44

Paris, Maghera s.a., Galerie Nataf 132

Paris, Réunion des Musées Nationaux 120-121, 128-129, 178-179

Paris, Réunion des Musées Nationaux, Arnaudet 113

Parma, Biblioteca Palatina, Ministero per i Beni Culturali e Ambientali, photography by Ernesto Greci 32-33, 52-53, 86-87, 149, 176-177

Pau, Musées des Beaux-Arts, photography by J. Ch. Poumeyrol 127

Rome, Galleria Nazionale d'Arte Moderna su concessione del Ministero per i Beni Culturali e Ambientali, photography by A. De Luca 14-15

Tolosa, Musée des Augustins 20-21

Venice, Biblioteca Nazionale Marciana, Ministero per i Beni Culturali e Ambientali, photography by Toso 10, 11, 13, 14, 18, 19, 26-27, 30, 31, 35, 39, 59, 63, 70, 71, 76, 81, 94, 99, 108, 110, 111, 112, 118, 134, 135, 138, 146, 147, 150, 151, 176, 182, 183, 185

Venice, Istituto di Storia dell'Arte della Fondazione G. Cini, photography by I. Candio 68-69

Venice, Fototeca Museo Correr 28, 36, 50, 60-61, 90-91, 158-159, 164, 165

Venice, Smith, Mark 51, 117, 174

Venice, Birri Flavio 11, 14, 25, 32, 34, 35, 37, 38, 62, 73, 77, 85, 95, 96, 99, 122, 124, 125, 138, 148, 154, 155, 163, 167, 168

Washington, Board of Trustees, National Gallery of Art 114-115

The images on pages 24, 40, 41, 53, 55, 104, 105, 162 were kindly provided by the author.